my **revision** notes

C000161469

Edexcel A-level History

THE BRITISH EXPERIENCE OF WARFARE

c.1790–1918

Alan Farmer
Peter Callaghan

HODDER
EDUCATION
AN HACHETTE UK COMPANY

Every effort has been made to trace all copyright holders, but if any have been inadvertently overlooked, the Publishers will be pleased to make the necessary arrangements at the first opportunity.

Although every effort has been made to ensure that website addresses are correct at time of going to press, Hodder Education cannot be held responsible for the content of any website mentioned in this book. It is sometimes possible to find a relocated web page by typing in the address of the home page for a website in the URL window of your browser.

Hachette UK's policy is to use papers that are natural, renewable and recyclable products and made from wood grown in sustainable forests. The logging and manufacturing processes are expected to conform to the environmental regulations of the country of origin.

Orders: please contact Bookpoint Ltd, 130 Milton Park, Abingdon, Oxon OX14 4SE. Telephone: +44 (0)1235 827720. Fax: +44 (0)1235 400401. Email education@bookpoint.co.uk Lines are open from 9 a.m. to 5 p.m., Monday to Saturday, with a 24-hour message answering service. You can also order through our website: www.hoddereducation.co.uk

ISBN: 978 1 5104 1813 4

© Alan Farmer 2018

First published in 2018 by
Hodder Education,
An Hachette UK Company
Carmelite House
50 Victoria Embankment
London EC4Y 0DZ

www.hoddereducation.co.uk

Impression number 10 9 8 7 6 5 4 3 2

Year 2022 2021 2020 2019 2018

Cover photo © Oleg Kulakov – stock.adobe.com

Illustrations by Integra

Typeset by Integra Software Services

Printed in Spain

A catalogue record for this title is available from the British Library.

My Revision Planner

REVISED

Part 2: Aspects in breadth: the changing role of government in preparing the nation for war, c1790–1918

REVISED

Introduction

About Paper 3

Paper 3 The British experience of warfare, c1790–1918, combines a depth study of Britain at war overseas with a broader thematic study of the changing role of government in preparing the nation for war, c1790–1918. Paper 3 tests you against two Assessment Objectives: AO1 and AO2.

AO1 tests your ability to:
- organise and communicate your own knowledge
- analyse and evaluate key features of the past
- make supported judgements
- deal with concepts of cause, consequence, change, continuity, similarity, difference and significance.

On Paper 1, AO1 tasks require you to write essays from your own knowledge.

AO2 tests your ability to:
- analyse and evaluate source material from the past
- explore the value of source material by considering its historical context.

On Paper 2, the AO2 task requires you to write an essay which analyses two sources from the period you have studied.

Paper 3 is worth 30 per cent of your A-level.

Structure

Paper 3 is structured around two themes and five key topics. The exam is divided into three sections, which relate to different aspects of your course.

Aspect of the course	Exam
Topic 1: Britain and the French Wars, 1793–1815	Section A (AO2) and Section B (AO1)
Topic 2: The Crimean War, 1854–56	
Topic 3: The second Boer War, 1899–1902	
Topic 4: Trench warfare on the Western Front, 1914–18	
Topic 5: War in the air, 1914–18	
Theme 1: Changes in organising the military	Section C (AO1)
Theme 2: Changes in the role of the people	

The exam

The Paper 3 exam lasts for 2 hours and 15 minutes and is divided into three sections.

Section A and Section B test the depth of your historical knowledge of the five topics:
- Section A requires you to answer one compulsory question concerning a single source. You should spend 15 to 20 minutes reading the source and planning your answer, and around 35 to 40 minutes writing the essay.
- Section B requires you to write one essay from a choice of two. As this is a depth paper, questions can be set on single events. Section B essays usually tests your knowledge on a shorter period than Section C. You should spend 35 to 40 minutes on Section B.

Section C requires you to answer one question from a choice of two. Questions in Section C will focus on the two themes and will cover at least 100 years. Questions can focus on either theme, or may test knowledge of both themes. You should spend 35 to 40 minutes on Section C.

How to use this book

This book has been designed to help you to develop the knowledge and skills necessary to succeed in this exam. Each section is made up of a series of topics organised into double-page spreads. On the left-hand page, you will find a summary of the key content you need to learn. Words in bold in the key content are defined in the glossary.

On the right-hand page, you will find exam-focused activities. Together, these two strands of the book will take you through the knowledge and skills essential for exam success.

There are three levels of exam-focused activities.
- Band 1 activities are designed to develop the foundational skills needed to pass the exam.
- Band 2 activities are designed to build on the skills developed in Band 1 activities and to help you achieve a C grade.
- Band 3 activities are designed to enable you to access the highest grades.

Some of the activities have answers or suggested answers online. These can be found at www.hoddereducation.co.uk/myrevisionnotes. These have the following symbol to indicate this:

Each section ends with an exam-style question and model high-level answer with commentary. This should give you guidance on what is required to achieve the top grades.

1 Britain and the French Wars, 1793–1815

Facing the French threat on land, 1793–1815

REVISED

The British Army, 1793–1815

Defeat in the American Revolutionary War (1775–83) tarnished the British Army's image.

The problem of recruitment

France, which had a system of conscription, was able to muster armies of hundreds of thousands. Britain could not match such numbers. In 1793 its army amounted to 40,000 men. Britain's regular soldiers were **volunteers**. Finding the requisite manpower was difficult because army pay was poor and discipline harsh.

Army officers

Traditionally most officers were from the landed gentry. Rich fathers bought sons an ensign's commission. The sons then bought promotions as vacancies appeared. Wealth mattered more than talent. However, the purchase system's impact can be exaggerated.

- Commissions were not purchased in the Royal Artillery or the Royal Engineers.
- The Duke of York introduced reforms ensuring that officers had to serve two years before they could purchase a captaincy and six years before they could become a major.
- Many officers led efficiently and courageously.

The army's composition

The army comprised three main branches – cavalry, infantry and artillery.

- By 1808, Britain had 20 cavalry regiments, in theory comprising some 900 men. However, regiments on campaign rarely mustered more than 650 men.
- By 1808, Britain had 103 infantry regiments. Most comprised two battalions. While one battalion served abroad, the other remained at home. The first battalion had about 950 officers and men, but disease and casualties meant that battalions often went into battle with 550 men. The infantry's main weapon was the Brown Bess musket which was only accurate up to 100 yards. Even experienced soldiers could rarely fire more than three shots a minute. In a defensive battle, British infantry stood in a line usually two ranks deep.

The French invariably attacked in columns – often 170 men wide and 24 ranks deep. While columns were an awesome spectacle, only the first two ranks could fire. Columns, therefore, rarely broke through a British line.

- British guns could hit a target at about 1,000 yards. They fired round shot, canister and shells. The army was short of heavy guns which could batter down the walls of fortresses.

The military situation, 1793–1809

After 1793 the army was engaged in campaigns in Europe and around the world.

The French Revolutionary War 1793–1802

The main British effort was against French possessions in the Caribbean. By 1798, British forces had captured several French, Spanish and Dutch islands. 40,000 soldiers died of yellow fever and other diseases.

British success in India

In 1797, **Arthur Wellesley** (see page 8) was sent on military duty to India. His brother Richard arrived in Calcutta as Governor-General the following year. Richard soon relied upon Arthur's military ability. In 1803, war broke out with the Mahratta Confederacy. In September 1803, Wellesley, with 7,000 men, attacked an Indian army of 40,000 at Assaye, winning a major victory. Two months later he triumphed at Argaum.

The Napoleonic War 1803–9

After 1803, British forces set about re-capturing colonies handed to France and its allies by the Treaty of Amiens (1802). Not all expeditions were successful.

- Efforts to capture Spanish colonies in South America ended in failure in 1807.
- In 1809, a 44,000-strong force was dispatched to capture Flushing and Antwerp. 4,000 died of disease on the island of Walchern before the army returned to Britain.

Quick quizzes at **www.hoddereducation.co.uk/myrevisionnotes**

Simple essay style

Below is a sample exam-style question. Use your own knowledge and the information on the opposite page to produce a plan for this question. Choose four general points and provide three pieces of specific information to support each general point. Once you have planned your essay, write the introduction and conclusion for it. The introduction should list the points to be discussed in the essay. The conclusion should summarise the key points and justify which point was the most important.

> To what extent did the British Army achieve its aims in the years 1793–1809?

Introducing an argument

Below are a sample exam-style question, a list of key points to be made in the essay and a simple introduction and conclusion for the essay. Read the question, the plan and the introduction and conclusion. Rewrite the introduction and conclusion in order to develop an argument.

> To what extent was the British Army a force to be reckoned with in the years 1793–1809?

Key points

- The size of the army
- The nature of the army
- The army's weaponry
- Military achievements, 1793–1802
- Military achievements, 1803–9

Introduction

The British Army had a poor reputation in 1793. The army's reputation was not greatly enhanced by its actions in the first fifteen years of the wars against France. The army was small in number, had difficulty recruiting and was commanded by men of wealth rather than talent.

Conclusion

Thus, the army did little to worry France in the years 1793–1809. It was unable to challenge France on the continent of Europe. Its only success came overseas — in India and the Caribbean. It was greatly in need of reform.

The role of Wellington in the defeat of the French

REVISED

The Peninsular War

Between 1808 and 1814, British troops were engaged in the Peninsular War, fighting for control of the Iberian Peninsula (essentially Spain and Portugal).

Early battles, 1808–9

In 1808, Spain and Portugal rose in revolt against French rule. Sir Arthur Wellesley commanded a 15,000-strong army which was sent to Portugal. After defeating a French army at Vimeiro, (French losses 2,000, British losses 720) he was replaced as commander by Sir Hew Dalrymple. Dalrymple was dismissed after agreeing that French soldiers in Portugal should be transported back to France on British ships.

In October 1808, Sir John Moore, the new commander of British forces in Portugal, marched into Spain hoping to cooperate with the Spanish in expelling the French from the country. But Napoleon invaded Spain in November with a force of 200,000 men and crushed Spanish forces. Moore's army retreated to Corunna where it fought French pursuers (16 January 1809). Moore was killed but the battle enabled 26,000 British troops to escape.

Wellesley returns

In April 1809, Wellesley was given command of British and Portuguese forces in Portugal.
- Within a few weeks he drove French troops from Oporto.
- In July, Wellesley's 20,000-strong army crossed into Spain. On 27–28 July, he defeated a 50,000-strong French army at Talavera in a fiercely fought battle.
- He was now forced to retreat to Portugal, where he remained on the defensive.
- Wellesley now became Viscount Wellington.

Massena's invasion of Portugal

In 1810, Marshal Massena advanced into Portugal with 65,000 men. Wellington fought a successful defensive battle at Busaco (27 September), before retreating towards Lisbon. Massena followed. In mid-October his forces reached the war's best kept secret – the lines of Torres Vedras. Wellington had ordered the construction of the lines – a network of formidable defences – in 1809. Massena was eventually forced to retreat into Spain in March 1811, having lost some 25,000 men. Portugal was now virtually free from French control.

The War: 1811–14

- Wellington's troops repelled two attacks on Fuentes de Onoro (May 1811).
- In early 1812, British forces captured Cuidad Rodrigo and Badajoz.
- Wellington won an important victory at Salamanca (22 July 1812) and entered Madrid in triumph.
- He reached Burgos in mid-September. But French armies threatened his rear, forcing him to retreat to Portugal.
- On 21 June 1813, Wellington defeated a 66,000-strong French army at Vitoria.
- He won a series of battles in the Pyrenees in July.
- In November, his army crossed into France and pressed northwards.
- In April 1814, Prussian, Russian and Austrian forces entered Paris. Napoleon abdicated and was exiled to the island of Elba.

Reasons for British success

- Wellington's leadership was vital. He never lost a battle.
- The British Army surpassed the French in every department – except numbers.
- Once Portuguese and Spanish troops were put under British command, they fought well.
- The Spanish and Portuguese people's stubborn resistance to French rule was crucially important.
- The Royal Navy conveyed supplies and transported troops.

The Battle of Waterloo

In 1815, Napoleon returned from exile and re-established his authority in France. The alliance powers of Britain, Russia, Austria and Prussia immediately declared war on France. Napoleon advanced northwards with 120,000 men hoping to annihilate the allied army, in (what is today) Belgium, commanded by Wellington, and the Prussian Army, commanded by Marshal Blücher. On 16 June, Napoleon defeated the Prussians at Ligny. Meanwhile, British and French forces fought a drawn battle at Quatre Bras. Believing that the Prussian Army had been crushed, Napoleon marched against Wellington. Wellington positioned his army on a low ridge near Waterloo. On 18 June, Napoleon attacked but Wellington's army held firm. As Prussian troops began arriving on the battlefield, Napoleon was defeated. Wellington's army suffered 15,000 casualties, Blücher's 7,000 and Napoleon's 25,000.

Mind map

Use the information on the opposite page to add detail to the mind map below, so that you gain a greater understanding of the achievements of Wellington after 1808.

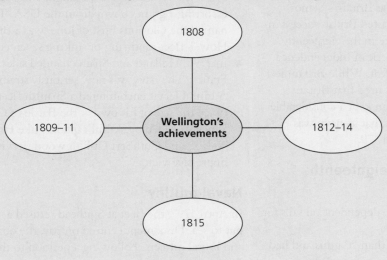

 Spectrum of significance

Below are a sample exam-style question and a list of general points which could be used to answer the question. Use your own knowledge and the information on the opposite page to reach a judgement about the importance of these general points to the question posed. Write numbers on the spectrum below to indicate their relative importance. Having done this, write a brief justification of your placement, explaining why some of these factors are more important than others. The resulting diagram could form the basis of an essay plan.

> To what extent was British success in the Peninsular War the result of Wellington's leadership?

←——————————————————————————————————→
Wellington's leadership vital   Other factors more important

1 Wellington's leadership qualities

2 The role of the British Army

3 The role of the Royal Navy

4 The resistance of the Spanish and Portuguese people

5 Napoleon's problems elsewhere in Europe

Facing the French at sea, 1793–1815

The Royal Navy in 1793

The navy had long been regarded as Britain's 'senior service'. Its strength had greatly assisted British success in most of the wars waged with France in the eighteenth century. However, the War of American Independence (1775–83) had ended in British defeat. While Britain lost its American colonies, the navy ensured that Britain escaped invasion. After 1783, Britain kept a considerable number of ships at sea. This meant that its navy was reasonably well prepared for war in 1793.

Naval warfare in the late eighteenth century

Ships were built of wood and were dependent on sails for movement.
- **Ships of the line** carried more than 70 guns and had crews of hundreds of men.
- Frigates, which carried fewer guns and men, were faster. They were in continual action, patrolling, scouting or conveying merchantmen.

The navy's strength was based on discipline and teamwork, especially the ability to fire guns swiftly and effectively.

Blockade

From 1793 onwards, the navy blockaded enemy ports, hoping to prevent ships getting out to sea. Two methods were used:
- a close blockade where the main fleet sailed near to the enemy port
- an open blockade where the main fleet was in a home port or miles away at sea, while frigates patrolled enemy ports, informing the main fleet if the enemy put to sea.

The naval war, 1793–7

- In 1793, Admiral Hood seized Toulon, France's main Mediterranean naval base. A French army soon forced him to abandon the port.
- The navy also blockaded French ports on the Atlantic coast. In 1794, Lord Howe fought a French fleet escorting a grain convoy from the USA. The battle, named the Glorious First of June, was a British victory, Howe's fleet capturing or sinking seven enemy ships.
- In 1796, Holland and Spain changed sides, joining France. The navy was now seriously strained. In 1797, Admiral Jervis encountered a Spanish fleet almost twice the size of his own at the Battle of Cape St Vincent. Aided by skilful captains, like **Horatio Nelson** and Cuthbert Collingwood, Jervis won an impressive victory.

Naval mutiny

In April 1797, the fleet at Spithead refused a command to put to sea. Discontent centred on pay, the quality of food and brutal officers. Following a petition to the **Admiralty**, the government agreed to raise wages. A fresh mutiny on 7 May, led by **petty officers**, the backbone of the navy, was well-handled by Lord Howe who guaranteed that the men's demands would be met.

On 12 May, sailors at the **Nore** mutinied. They had more far-reaching demands including the power of veto over officers. The Nore mutineers were joined by the North Sea Fleet. For a few weeks Britain seemed defenceless. The government took steps to isolate and starve the mutineers. The mutiny ended in mid-June when moderate sailors wrested control from the radicals. Twenty-nine mutineers were executed.

For a few weeks, it seemed that the navy's most valuable asset – its discipline – was on the verge of collapse. The navy's reputation was restored at the Battle of Camperdown (October 1797) when Admiral Duncan's North Sea Fleet destroyed a Dutch fleet.

The situation in 1797

Despite Camperdown, Britain's outlook seemed bleak:
- French invasion remained a serious threat
- a large French army and fleet at Toulon was preparing to sail – no one was sure where.

! Complete the paragraph   a

Below are a sample exam-style question and a paragraph written in answer to this question. The paragraph contains a point and a concluding explanatory link back to the question, but lacks examples. Complete the paragraph, adding examples in the space provided.

How accurate is it to say that the Royal Navy ruled the waves in the years 1793–7?

> The naval mutinies in 1797 were a threat to Britain's naval supremacy.
>
> _____
>
> _____

> Accordingly, for a few weeks in mid-1797, the Royal Navy did not rule the waves and Britain might well have been invaded.

! Eliminate irrelevance   a

Below are a sample exam-style question and a paragraph written in answer to this question. Read the paragraph and identify parts of the paragraph that are not directly relevant to the question. Draw a line through the information that is not relevant and justify your deletions in the margin.

How accurate is it to say that the Royal Navy's supremacy in the years 1793-7 was based on the skill of its naval leaders?

> In 1795 Sir John Jervis took over command in the Mediterranean, replacing Hood. Jervis, who loathed inefficiency, set about whipping the fleet into shape. He forged an excellent relationship with those officers (like Nelson) whom he trusted and respected. In 1796 the situation deteriorated when the Netherlands and Spain changed sides, joining France against Britain. The Royal Navy, now facing far more enemy ships, was seriously strained. The main British fleet was stationed at Spithead (off Portsmouth), leaving just fifteen battleships to blockade Brest, where double that number of French ships were preparing to break out. Jervis, meanwhile, stationed the bulk of his force off Cadiz, facing the main Spanish fleet. On 14 February 1797 Jervis's fleet encountered a Spanish force almost twice the size of his own at the Battle of Cape St Vincent. Confident in the skills of his men, Jervis attacked, his ships cutting through the enemy line. Jervis knew that the Royal Navy's strength was the discipline and teamwork of his men. While some operated guns, others worked aloft, furling and unfurling sails. The gunners were particularly well-trained. The speed at which guns fired usually determined the outcome of naval battles. Jervis's seamen could unleash a broadside every minute and a half — much faster than their enemies. Nelson played a major role. Acting with speed and courage, he boarded and captured the much larger San Josef. Jervis won a great victory, capturing four enemy ships and driving the rest back into Cadiz. He was now ennobled as the Earl of St Vincent and soon became the head of the Channel Fleet.

The role of Nelson in defeating the French

Horatio Nelson inspired men and fellow officers, winning their trust and affection. His hallmark as a commander was simple: get in close to the enemy and let British gunnery do the talking.

The Battle of the Nile, 1798

In 1798, Napoleon Bonaparte left Toulon with thirteen battleships and 280 transports carrying nearly 50,000 men. His destination was Egypt. Nelson was given the task of destroying the French fleet. He found the French fleet at the mouth of the River Nile on 1 August. While both fleets were similar in strength, superior British gunnery devastated the French. Only two French ships escaped. The stunning victory enabled the Royal Navy to regain control of the Mediterranean.

The Battle of Copenhagen, 1801

In 1801, Admiral Parker commanded a Baltic fleet sent to Copenhagen to deal with the potential threat from Denmark's fleet. Parker gave Nelson, his second-in-command, the task of leading the attack on Copenhagen (2 April 1801). Nelson sailed into a narrow strip of water, lined with Danish warships, gun batteries on rafts and shore forts. At one stage, worried at Danish resistance, Parker signalled Nelson to discontinue the action. Nelson ignored the signal and proceeded to force Denmark's Crown Prince to agree to a truce. Three Danish ships were sunk and twelve captured.

The situation, 1803–5

In 1803, Nelson was given command of the Mediterranean Fleet. His main task was to keep watch on the French fleet in Toulon, commanded by Villeneuve. In 1804, the situation deteriorated when Spain allied with France. The two countries had 102 battleships. The Royal Navy had 83. If Napoleon could concentrate his ships in the English Channel, a French invasion was a serious possibility.

Napoleon's plan was for Villeneuve to evade Nelson, lure him to the Caribbean, lose him and sail back to Europe, uniting with other French and Spanish fleets. This combined fleet would enable Napoleon's army at Boulogne to invade Britain. In April 1805, Villeneuve's fleet left Toulon. Nelson, with fewer ships, gave chase. Failing to catch up with Villeneuve in the Caribbean, he sailed home. In July, a British fleet under Sir Robert Calder intercepted Villeneuve off Cape Finisterre. Most of Villeneuve's fleet escaped, eventually sailing to Cadiz. Nelson and Calder's fleets joined Cornwallis off Brest, lifting the invasion threat.

The Battle of Trafalgar, 1805

Nelson was now given command of the fleet off Cadiz. On 19 October, Villeneuve left Cadiz for Italy. Nelson gave chase. He had 27 battleships, 17,000 men and 2,148 guns. Villeneuve's French-Spanish fleet had 33 battleships, 30,000 men and 2,568 guns. The two fleets came to battle on 21 October. Nelson formed his fleet into two **divisions**, one led by himself in *HMS Victory*, the other by Collingwood. The two columns shattered the enemy line and won a massive victory, taking eighteen enemy battleships. Nelson, shot by a French sharpshooter, died of his wounds.

The impact of Trafalgar

After 1805, the navy was not seriously challenged by the French. It remained active.

- In 1807, Britain banned trade with any ports complying with Napoleon's **Berlin Decrees**. British ships stopped and searched any neutral ship suspected of trading with the enemy.
- The navy transported troops and supplies to Spain and Portugal.
- The navy enabled Britain to seize French and Dutch colonies.
- British frigates terrorised European coastlines, tying down large numbers of enemy troops.
- The navy fought a naval war with the USA (1812–14), eventually blockading most American ports.

Spot the mistake **a**

Below are a sample exam-style question and an introductory paragraph written in answer to this question. Why does the paragraph not get into Level 4? Once you have identified the mistake, rewrite the paragraph so that it displays the qualities of Level 4. The mark scheme on page 103 will help you.

> To what extent did Horatio Nelson deserve the acclaim he was accorded in the years 1798 to 1805?

> Nelson's victory at the Battle of the Nile greatly enhanced his standing. He won a stunning victory over the French fleet. Of the thirteen French ships only two escaped and Napoleon was trapped in Egypt. The Royal Navy again controlled the Mediterranean.

 Develop the detail **a**

Below are a sample exam-style question and an introductory paragraph written in answer to this question. The paragraph contains a limited amount of detail. Annotate the paragraph to add additional detail to the answer.

> To what extent did the Battle of Trafalgar save Britain?

> The battle of Trafalgar was a decisive victory. But it did not prevent a French invasion. Nor did it have much impact on the remainder of the war of the Third Coalition. Nevertheless, after Trafalgar the Royal Navy achieved an aura of invincibility.

The impact of the French Wars on the British economy, 1793–1815

The British economy

Britain's growing economy enabled the government to finance the war. Between 1783 and 1802, Britain's economy grew at an annual rate of nearly six per cent, a greater pace than at any time during the previous century.

Industrial growth

Britain's industries made spectacular advances during the war.

- Cotton production increased threefold between 1793 and 1813.
- Iron and steel manufacturing output increased fourfold during the same period.
- While most of British industry was still powered by watermills, steam power was growing in importance. By 1805, 112 steam engines were operating in London.

Agricultural growth

Throughout the war, Britain had to import grain from Europe and North America. High wartime prices for foodstuffs created prosperity for farmers and encouraged investment in farming. Common land and wasteland was cultivated and corn output increased by over a fifth between 1790 and 1810. The Board of Agriculture and Internal Improvement, managed by its industrious chairman John Sinclair and able secretary Arthur Young, encouraged improvements in breeding and crop rotation.

Commerce and finance

During the eighteenth century, largely thanks to the Industrial and Agricultural revolutions, Britain had developed a strong and resilient financial system, in contrast to France's antiquated and inefficient system.

The City of London played a vital role in providing funds for the war. Leading financiers, such as Nathan Rothschild, arranged large loans to fund Britain's military campaigns and to subsidise Britain's allies, especially Russia and Austria. In 1815, the National Debt stood at over £1 billion.

Canals

Britain began to develop its canal network in the eighteenth century. That development continued during the war years. The Grand Junction Canal, for example, which joined the Midlands to London, was started in 1795. It was operational by 1805. The opening up of more canals greatly reduced the cost of transporting bulky goods.

British trade

Given that a large proportion of government income derived from customs duties, overseas trade was vital to the war effort. Cotton textiles led the export drive. By 1815, their value was six times greater than in 1793. Exports of manufactured goods also increased considerably. Despite Napoleon's **Continental System**, between 1808 and 1810, trade flourished as new markets were found in South America and the Caribbean. But between late 1810 and 1812, trade declined. Poor harvests and war with the USA added to the economic gloom. However, after Napoleon's defeat in Russia, the Continental System began to collapse, ensuring that British goods were again shipped to Europe.

The East India Company

The East India Company greatly assisted Britain's war effort.

- It exported great quantities of goods to India and the Far East.
- Its ships brought back vital materials, including saltpetre, an essential ingredient in gunpowder manufacture.
- Its ships were chartered to transport troops abroad.
- It swelled the government's coffers through the payment of high duties on Asian imports, especially tea.

Military production

The critical task for British politicians and administrators was to translate the buoyant economy and the resulting wealth into an efficient military machine. Throughout the war, the government had its own military establishments, producing warships, weapons and gunpowder. However, state ordnance yards and dockyards lacked the capacity to achieve the increased levels of production that were required. The private sector came to the government's aid. Privately owned shipyards, foundries and factories, working on government contracts, ultimately built more ships and manufactured more weapons than the state.

The situation by 1815

If anything, Britain's economy was strengthened by the war. By 1815, manufacturing and mining industries were thriving, shipyards were busy and new markets abroad had opened up.

Simple essay style

Below is a sample exam-style question. Use your own knowledge and the information on the opposite page to produce a plan for this question. Choose four general points and provide three pieces of specific information to support each general point. Once you have planned your essay, write the introduction and conclusion for it. The introduction should list the points to be discussed in the essay. The conclusion should summarise the key points and justify which point was the most important.

> How accurate is it to say that the British economy benefited from the wars against France in the years 1793–1815?

 Support or challenge?

Below is a sample exam-style question which asks how far you agree with a specific statement. Below this is a series of general statements which are relevant to the question. Using your own knowledge and the information on the opposite page, decide whether these statements support or challenge the statement in the question and tick the appropriate box.

> 'The strength of its economy enabled Britain to win the **French Revolutionary** and Napoleonic Wars.' How far do you agree with this statement about Britain's success in the years 1793–1815?

	Support	Challenge
Cotton production increased threefold between 1793 and 1813.		
Iron and steel manufacturing output increased fourfold between 1793 and 1813.		
The British government was able to pay for the cost of the war.		
Napoleon's Continental System did not unduly damage the British economy.		
British success in the French Wars was mainly due to the Royal Navy.		
Canal development continued through the war years.		
The East India Company greatly assisted the British war effort.		
High wartime prices for foodstuffs created prosperity for farmers and encouraged investment in farming.		

Why did Britain triumph?

Military factors

Military success contributed considerably to Britain's success.

The navy's role

The navy enabled Britain to escape invasion, expand its trade and continue to prosecute the war. 'If anyone wishes to know the history of this war', said Wellington, 'I will tell them it is our maritime supremacy.'

The army's role

Given its relatively small size, the army performed well. When commanded by Wellington, it was never defeated. Napoleon said his defeat could be traced to the Peninsular War, which was a constant drain on French resources.

Foreign support

Without the military assistance of Russia, Prussia and Austria, it is hard to see how Britain could have won the Napoleonic War.

Other factors

While its navy and army can take most of the credit, British victory was the result of many other factors.

British governments

The British parliamentary system, for all its faults, proved itself better at waging war than Napoleon's dictatorship. Between 1793 and 1815, there were six prime ministers, ten foreign secretaries, seven secretaries of state for war and ten first lords of the admiralty. Not all these men were particularly talented. But Britain did produce some able wartime leaders, not least Prime Ministers William Pitt the Younger (1793–1801 and 1804–6), Spencer Perceval (1809–12) and Lord Liverpool (1812–27).

While the Tory Party supported the war, many Whigs favoured appeasing France and making peace. But in 1794, some 60 moderate Whigs, led by the Duke of Portland, joined the Tory government's side. This realignment kept the Whigs from power for the next forty years except for one administration in 1806–7.

The British economy

Britain's economic strength underpinned the entire British war effort. By 1815, manufacturing and mining industries were thriving, shipyards were busy, agricultural prices were high and new markets abroad had opened up.

Funding war

Britain's buoyant economy ensured that governments were able to find sufficient funds to pay for the wars. At least 21 goods and services were newly taxed during the war, including windows and dogs. In 1799, a graduated income tax was introduced for the first time in Britain's history. Before 1793, around £18 million a year was raised in taxes. An additional £12 million on average was extracted every year between 1793 and 1815.

Government bureaucracy

Corruption and inefficiency in government was a major problem. But after 1806, financial and administrative reform gathered pace. Ancient customs were abandoned, money saved and sinecures diminished as younger, more able men rose to the top.

Popular support for the war

The government, churches and local authorities did their best to maintain support for the war effort. Various forms of propaganda – newspapers, pamphlets, posters, sermons – were used. Most Britons, however, fearing the prospect of French invasion, already supported the war. The richer classes were prepared to pay increased taxes and provide military and naval officers, while the willingness of the poorer classes to join the armed forces meant that Britain did not have to introduce conscription. The propaganda produced by the authorities generally reached those who already supported the war effort and, while there were occasional fears that revolution might spread across the Channel, most Britons were committed to achieving victory.

Mind map

Use the information on the opposite page to add detail to the mind map below. This should provide you with a greater understanding of causes for British success in the French Revolutionary and Napoleonic Wars.

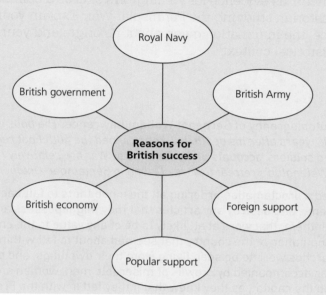

RAG – rate the timeline

Below are a sample exam-style question and a timeline. Read the question, study the timeline and, using three coloured pens, put a Red, Amber or Green star next to the events to show:

Red: events and policies that have no relevance to the question.

Amber: events and policies that have some significance to the question.

Green: events and policies that are directly relevant to the question.

To what extent was the entire British population involved in the wars against France in the years 1793–1815?

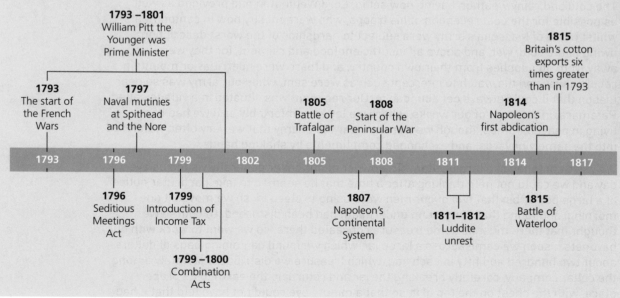

Exam focus

Below are a question, a source and a sample answer. Read all three, including the comments around the answer.

Assess the value of Source 1 as evidence for Wellington's skill as a commander and as evidence for a historian studying the Peninsular War. Explain your answer, using the source, the information given about its origin and your own knowledge about the historical context.

SOURCE 1

This extract is from The Autobiography of Sergeant William Lawrence. *The book was published in London in 1886, years after his death. Lawrence joined the 40th Foot regiment in 1804. Non-commissioned soldiers' accounts of the Peninsular War are relatively rare. In this extract, he describes Wellington's retreat towards Lisbon in September-October 1810.*

Lord Wellington had issued a proclamation ordering all the inhabitants to fall back on the approach of the enemy, and destroy any articles that they might possess and were not able to carry with them, that were at all likely to be of any value to the enemy; and so thousands of the population of the country that seemed about to fall within the bounds of the enemy's marches were to be seen flying from their dwellings, and our army during its retreat was accompanied by crowds of miserable men, women and children, all eager to reach the capital, as they knew that if they fell in with the French, they would be treated as some had been before, with all the barbarities of an atrocious enemy [...]

[...] From Leiria we went on further to Torres Vedras, which we gained after a long, tedious, and impressive march, and there we took up our position at some fine breastworks which Lord Wellington had for some time previous ordered to be thrown up by the Portuguese peasantry in case of the retreat of our army. Now we found how much we needed them, for on the 10th of October the French came in sight of our strong position, where we had drawn up, determined that they should not proceed one step farther towards Lisbon.

Massena was rather surprised at our strength which was quite unexpected by him. He had thought of driving the English into the sea, but he now found his mistake, so encamped about a mile from our position.

The cold and rainy weather, having now set in, Lord Wellington had provided as well as possible for the best reception of his troops, who were mostly now in cantonments, whilst those of Massena's army were subject to hardships of the worst description, owing to the cold, wet, and above all insufficient food and raiment, for they were far away from all supplies from their own country, and there were guerrillas or mountain rebels always on the watch to intercept such as were sent, while our army was so near Lisbon that it could always get abundance. Our regiment was situated in a village called Patamara, in the front of our works, where we lay as comfortably as if we had been living in peaceful times, though we were so near the enemy that we very often wandered into the same vineyards, and exchanged compliments by shaking hands.

We were cantoned in a large cellar... The owner of our cellar generally visited us every day and we could not help thinking after a time that he seemed to take particular notice of a large box or bin that two of our men were using to sleep in, so we moved it one morning, and found that the ground underneath had been disturbed. Of course we thought that there must be some treasure concealed there, so we went to work with our bayonets... soon we came across a large jar, which we found containing bags of dollars, about two hundred and fifty in each bag, which treasure we distributed privately among the cellar company, carefully breaking the jar and returning the earth to its proper place, with the chest on the top of it, so that a minute eye could not have told that it had been disturbed.

The extract provides limited value to a historian examining Wellington's skill as a commander. Lawrence gives us an ordinary soldier's perspective of the retreat south after Wellington's victory at Busaco on 27 September 1810. He has relatively little to say about Wellington. He does provides information about Wellington's efforts to persuade the Portuguese civilians to retreat with the army towards Lisbon. He comments on the misery of the Portuguese civilians caught up in the events but gives the impression that Wellington's proclamation was for the civilians' own good. Lawrence does not stress that Wellington was conducting a 'scorched earth' policy, intending to empty the land of food so that the Massena's army would be unable to feed itself over the winter.

The source also understates the importance of the Lines of Torres Vedras. They are described as simply 'some fine breastworks'. They were rather more than that. The lines of Torres Vedras were a network of formidable defences some 20–30 miles north of Lisbon that consisted of three defensive rings. The 26 mile northern-most line, which ran from the Atlantic to the River Tagus, consisted of linked forts and earthworks covering the passes through to Lisbon. The Royal Navy protected the Atlantic flank and gunboats on the River Tagus made it hard for the French to cross. A second – stronger – line of defences was built behind the first. A third line would protect the British Army if it was forced back to Lisbon and had to escape by sea from Portugal. They were surely worth more attention than Lawrence provides.

Lawrence does praise Wellington for ensuring the troops were provided with good quarters – a cellar in Lawrence's case – and well-provided with supplies. This was indeed the case. British ships provided enough supplies to feed Wellington's army, the people of Lisbon and the refugees. Massena and the French, by contrast, were soon, as Lawrence says, 'subject to hardships of the worst description'. Wellington's main army, nearly 60,000 strong, was deployed behind the lines, ready to concentrate against a French thrust wherever it might come. It never came. Massena thought the defences were too strong to attack but his pride would not allow him to retreat. Meanwhile his army grew desperately short of food. In mid-November, he finally withdrew 30 miles to positions stretching between Santarem and Rio Maior, well-protected by earthworks and marshes. Wellington followed and the besieged now became the besiegers. Wellington's generalship in 1810 was of the highest order. This does not come across in Lawrence's account.

The source is more useful to historians studying the Peninsular War as a whole rather than Wellington as an individual. While there are many officer accounts of the war (diaries, letters, published reminiscences), accounts by non-commissioned men are far fewer as such men lacked the methods or means to record events in these ways. Lawrence's recollections were almost certainly written down long after the events he describes, so are scarcely 'primary'. It is also not certain how literate Lawrence was. It is likely his autobiography was ghost-written, and the writer may have put words in Lawrence's mouth. Recollections of past attitudes, concerns and actions are not necessarily accurate, and memories can – indeed usually are – coloured by later events.

This is a strong introduction. It shows an understanding of both the source and Wellington's campaign in Portugal in the autumn of 1810.

This paragraph displays excellent knowledge of Wellington's Lines of Torres Vedras. Commenting on a source's omissions is a high order skill. It is indeed surprising that Lawrence did not say more about the Lines – or his feelings when reaching them.

This paragraph again shows excellent background knowledge of the situation in 1810. Lawrence, who lived through the events, says little about the situation – and most of what he does say could have been picked up much later.

There are problems with the source, including its provenance, but it nevertheless remains useful simply because accounts by ordinary soldiers are relatively rare.

With all these caveats, Lawrence's memories have some value. His attitudes to both the Portuguese and French seem fairly typical of British soldiers. He expresses some sympathy for Portuguese civilians who have been forced to leave their homes but does not seem to particularly respect them – he was prepared to rob one of his savings. His attitude to the French is similarly ambivalent. In one paragraph he describes their actions as barbarous and calls them an 'atrocious enemy'. Yet a few sentences later, he talks about meeting French soldiers in vineyards and shaking hands.

Lawrence's main concern seems to be creature comforts – especially food and shelter. He was well-housed (albeit in a large cellar) and so well fed that his company had no need to make use of a quantity of wheat they found in their cellar. It is perhaps surprising that Lawrence says little of the march from Busaco to the Lines, except that it was 'long, tedious and impressive'. Some of those who wrote at the time were highly critical of Wellington for retreating. Many believed the British Army should have stood and fought. We have no idea what Lawrence thought.

Lawrence also says relatively little about events on the march south. The main action he describes reads as a kind of jape – stealing from his Portuguese 'landlord', the kind of incident that seems to have been commonplace among the troops of Wellington's army. Lawrence was stealing considerable quantities of money from an erstwhile ally however, something that was undoubtedly a capital crime. Lawrence seems proud of what he and his company had done, but it is worth remembering that his actions deprived a man – an ally – of a considerable part of his wealth.

It would be quite easy to say that the last paragraph of the source is of little use to the historian. Yet arguably it is the most important paragraph in the source. It tells us of something that Lawrence actually did – unlike most of the other paragraphs. The story does not reflect well on the man or the rest of his company. But it gives us a 'feel' of the actions and attitudes of the men of Wellington's army. No one has ever tried to argue they were saints. Wellington himself was prone to describe his men as 'the scum of the earth'. (But he also respected their fighting qualities and did his best to protect them.) Here is evidence that suggests that British soldiers were indeed thieves at heart and were quite happy to disobey Wellington's orders (not to upset or steal from Britain's Portuguese allies) if they thought they had a chance of getting away with their 'crime'. It should be said that Lawrence does not even seem to consider what he has done to be a crime. He is proud to recount the tale – a tale in which British soldiers cheated their Portuguese allies. It may be that there were hundreds of similar incidents as a result of thousands of British soldiers living cheek by jowl with the Portuguese people. We don't know about them. We do know about this!

This is a short but incisive paragraph. It does well to pick out Lawrence's somewhat ambivalent attitude to both the Portuguese and the French.

This paragraph very much links to the promised structure – attitudes, concerns and actions. The candidate spots the emphasis on food and shelter. The sin of omission – little comment on the events of the retreat – is also well made.

Now actions! A short but important and effective paragraph.

A number of incisive points are made about the value of the source to historians and about the nature of Wellington's troops. A strong finish.

This is a clear Level 5 answer. The candidate shows an excellent understanding of the source, its context and the Peninsular War. The candidate displays ability to analyse the source in a sophisticated way with regard to both lines of enquiry. He/she is able to use his/her contextual knowledge to make a number of important inferences and judgements with relation to the source.

Linking factors

One of the reasons why this essay is so successful is that it draws links between the factors it discusses. Read through the essay again and highlight the points at which the factors are discussed.

2 The Crimean War, 1854–6

In March 1854, Britain and France declared war on Russia, triggering the first major European war since the defeat of Napoleon in 1815.

Facing the Russian threat in the Crimea

The British Army in 1854

Soon after war was declared, a 26,000-strong British army sailed for the Crimea. Its spirited appearance camouflaged significant problems in command and organisation.

The influence of Wellington

Wellington, Commander-in-Chief in 1827–8 and again from 1842–52, exercised massive influence over military affairs. He believed that what had served the army well in the past was the surest guarantee of continuing success. He was convinced that calls for army reforms were merely demands for cuts in military spending.

The military commanders

Lord Raglan, head of the British expeditionary force, had served on Wellington's staff in the Peninsular War and had subsequently been Wellington's military secretary. No one doubted his administrative ability or bravery. Unfortunately, he had seen no active service since 1815 and had never commanded an army. Only one of Raglan's five infantry divisional commanders was under 60, and he, the Duke of Cambridge, was Queen Victoria's cousin who had not seen action before. Chief Engineer Sir John Burgoyne was 72. Only two divisional commanders had led anything larger than a battalion into action.

While there were signs of growing professionalism among sections of the officer corps, the system of buying commissions ensured that wealth often triumphed over ability. Officers were drawn principally from the landed gentry and from military families.

Military administration

A variety of people and departments were responsible for military administration. These included the Secretary of State for War and the Colonies, the Secretary-at-War, the Commander-in-Chief, the Adjutant-General, the Quartermaster-General, the Home Secretary, the Ordnance Office and the **Commissariat**. Such a cumbersome structure produced delays and inertia.

The problem of manpower

Poor conditions of service meant the army had difficulty attracting sufficient recruits.
- Most barracks were overcrowded and insanitary.
- Soldiers' pay was poor.
- Service overseas exacted a heavy toll in life and health.
- Soldiers could still be flogged for a variety of 'crimes'.
- Infantry served for 21 years; cavalry 24 years.

The situation by 1854

Given that no-one had expected British troops to be involved in a major European war, little thought had been given to **staff work** and administrative co-ordination. Yet in 1854, the army was expected to achieve a quick and comprehensive victory over Russia. It is, perhaps, a tribute to the professionalism and bravery of many of its officers and men that the army fought as well as it did. The fact that the infantry were armed with **rifled muskets** gave British troops a huge advantage. The British Enfield rifle was accurate at over 400 yards (366 m); most Russian muskets had an effective range of under 100 yards.

(i) You're the examiner

Below are a sample exam question and a paragraph written in answer to the question. Read the paragraph and the mark scheme provided on page 103. Describe what level you would award the paragraph. Write the level below along with a justification for your choice.

To what extent was the British Army ready for war in 1854?

> By 1854, there were signs of growing professionalism among sections of the officer corps. But actual experience of command was confined to colonial wars and many officers had seen no active service at all. The system of buying commissions ensured that wealth often triumphed over ability. In 1814, the greatly enlarged British Army had been led by men mainly from the professional classes. However, by 1854, the much smaller army was led by officers drawn principally from the landed gentry and from families with a military tradition. While most had a high sense of duty, some joined the army because it provided them with a fashionable, and not too strenuous, existence.

Level:

Reason for choosing this level and this mark

_____

_____

(i) Develop the detail   a

Below are a sample exam-style question and a paragraph written in answer to this question. The paragraph contains a limited amount of detail. Annotate the paragraph to add additional detail to the answer.

How accurate is it to say that the British Army sent to the Crimea in 1854 was 'the finest army that has ever left these shores'?

> The quality of British military command was a cause of concern. Lord Raglan, appointed to command the Crimean Army, was 55 and had not seen active service since 1815. Only one of Raglan's divisional commanders was under 60.

The impact of the battles of Alma and Balaclava

The battle of Alma, September 1854

In mid-September 1854, 63,000 British and French troops landed unopposed in the Crimea and marched towards Sebastopol, an important naval base on the Black Sea. At the River Alma the allied forces encountered a Russian army commanded by Prince Alexander Menshikov occupying a strong defensive position on the heights above the river. Fierce fighting ensued, which forced the outnumbered Russian forces to withdraw. Raglan wanted the allies to march at once to take Sebastopol, but the cautious French high command refused. This decision allowed the Russians to regroup and continue the war into 1855.

Alma highlighted some weaknesses among the British troops:
● Some officers provided poor leadership.
● Many of the troops were untrained.
Nevertheless, the British Army as a whole had fought well.

The battle of Balaclava, October 1854

After a difficult march southward, the allied forces laid siege to Sebastopol in October, a decision which gave the Russians time to improve its defences. Raglan's army took up positions around Balaclava.

On 25 October, a Russian army advanced towards Balaclava. Russian cavalry were driven back by the Heavy Brigade. But a misunderstood order resulted in the Light Brigade attacking well-defended Russian artillery. Of the 664 men who charged, 110 were killed, 130 wounded and 58 taken prisoner.

The battle of Inkerman, November 1854

Balaclava had boosted the Russians' morale and by early November they had gained a large number of reinforcements. On 5 November, the Russians attacked Inkerman Ridge. Small units of British infantry fought much larger numbers of Russians. The arrival of French troops led to the Russians retreating, having suffered 11,000 casualties. The British lost 597 killed and 1,860 wounded, the French, 130 killed and 750 wounded. Although the allied armies had fought magnificently, they were no nearer capturing Sebastopol.

The siege of Sebastopol, 1854–5

The Crimean winter 1854–5 was cold and wet. Given the shortage of tents and the lack of firewood, men were unable to cook or stay dry and warm.

The problem of transport

Transporting supplies from Britain to Balaclava (4,000 miles; 6,500 km) was easy. Transport from Balaclava to the siege lines (just six miles; 9.5 km) proved more difficult. Incompetent Commissariat officials failed to provide the troops with essential supplies of food, fuel, tents and clothing. Balaclava became a place of nightmarish chaos.

The medical situation

Soldiers suffered from **cholera**, **scurvy**, **typhus**, **typhoid** and **dysentery**. Hospital tents and medicines were scarce and the filthy and overcrowded hospitals at Balaclava and Scutari provided little comfort. By late January 1855, the British Army was only 11,000 strong, while the sick and wounded totalled 23,000. However, as spring approached, the administrative chaos lessened and supplies were better distributed, leading to a marked decline in the number of deaths.

The capture of Sebastopol, September 1855

There was little allied movement against Sebastopol during the winter of 1854–5. British and French attacks in June 1855 failed and on 28 June, Raglan, overworked and dispirited, died of dysentery. In September, after more allied attacks, the Russians abandoned Sebastopol.

The role of Lord Raglan

Raglan's command of the British forces was strongly criticized by contemporaries:
● Raglan used many of the same methods in the Crimea as Wellington had used forty years earlier against Napoleon. Many believed Raglan preferred traditional methods of warfare rather than seeking to innovate.
● The dreadful conditions experienced by Raglan's troops were caused by the incompetence of commanders who mismanaged the delivery of supplies to Balaclava and the Sebastopol siege lines. Raglan was blamed, however.
● Raglan was unable to persuade the allies to mount an all-out attack on Sebastopol. The siege warfare they undertook instead lengthened the war by many months. This was perhaps Raglan's biggest failing.

Add the content

Below is a sample exam question with the accompanying source. Having read the question and the source, complete the following activity.

> Assess the value of Source 1 for revealing 1) information about the Charge of the Light Brigade and 2) the attitudes of William Howard Russell. Explain your answer using the source, the information given about its origin and your own knowledge about the historical context.

First, look for aspects of the source that refer to events and/or discussions that were going on around the time that the source was written. Underline the key phrases and write a brief description of the context in the margin next to the source. Draw an arrow from the key phrase to the context. Try and find at least three key phrases from the source.

Tip: look at the information above the source. You should contextualise this too. Pay particular attention to the date on which the source was written.

SOURCE 1

This source was written by William Howard Russell, a reporter for The Times, *who accompanied the British Army to the Crimea. Historian Christopher Hibbert states his reports were 'eagerly awaited and avidly read by almost the entire literate population'. This extract was published in* The Times *on 14 November 1854. It led to Alfred Lord Tennyson writing his famous poem* The Charge of the Light Brigade.

HEIGHTS BEFORE SEBASTOPOL, OCTOBER 25 1854

If the exhibition of the most brilliant valour, of the excess of courage, and of a daring which would have reflected lustre on the best days of chivalry can afford consolation for the disaster of today, we can have no reason to regret the melancholy loss which we sustained in a contest with a savage and barbarous enemy.

I shall proceed to describe, to the best of my power, what occurred under my own eyes, and to state the facts which I have heard from men whose veracity is unimpeachable, reserving to myself the right of private judgement in making public and in suppressing the details of what occurred on this memorable day.

At 11.00 our Light Cavalry Brigade rushed to the front...The Russians opened on them with guns from the redoubts on the right, with volleys of musketry and rifles. They swept proudly past, glittering in the morning sun in all the pride and splendour of war. We could hardly believe the evidence of our senses. Surely that handful of men were not going to charge an army in position? Alas! It was but too true – their desperate valour knew no bounds, and far indeed was it removed from its so-called better part – discretion. They advanced in two lines, quickening the pace as they closed towards the enemy. A more fearful spectacle was never witnessed than by those who, without the power to aid, beheld their heroic countrymen rushing to the arms of sudden death. At the distance of 1200 yards the whole line of the enemy belched forth from thirty iron mouths, a flood of smoke and flame through which hissed the deadly balls. Their flight was marked by instant gaps in our ranks, the dead men and horses, by steeds flying wounded or riderless across the plain. The first line was broken – it was joined by the second, they never halted or checked their speed in an instant. With diminished ranks, thinned by those thirty guns, which the Russians had laid with the most deadly accuracy, with a halo of flashing steel above their heads, and with a cheer which was many a noble fellow's death cry, they flew into the smoke of the batteries, but ere they were lost from view, the plain was strewn with their bodies and with the carcasses of horses. They were exposed to an oblique fire from the batteries on the hills on both sides, as well as to a direct fire of musketry.

Through the clouds of smoke we could see the sabres flashing as they rode up to the guns and dashed between them, cutting down the gunners as they stood...To our delight, we saw them returning, after breaking through a column of Russian infantry and scattering them like chaff, when the flank fire of the battery on the hill swept them down, scattered and broken as they were. Wounded men and dismounted troopers flying towards us told the sad tale – demigods could not have done what they had failed to do.

The effectiveness of Florence Nightingale and Mary Seacole

Nightingale's work in the Crimean War

Born into an upper-class family, **Nightingale** decided – remarkably – to devote herself to nursing. Women of her background did not become nurses.

Scutari

Hearing reports about horrific hospital conditions in Turkey and the Crimea, Nightingale volunteered to help. With the authorisation of War Secretary Sidney Herbert, she recruited 38 female nurses. In November 1854, she and her team arrived at Scutari. They found sick and wounded soldiers being badly cared for by overworked male staff.

Dr John Hall, Raglan's Principal Medical Officer, and his doctors, initially allowed Nightingale's nurses to undertake only menial duties. But as hospital numbers increased, Nightingale's influence grew, particularly as she managed a charitable fund of £30,000, which she used to purchase medical necessities. She also worked energetically, ensuring that wards were cleaned, fresh bed linen was available and better food was provided.

Nightingale's reputation

Nightingale became a national heroine. In many ways she was – and is – wrongly depicted.

- Soldiers' wives had long tended soldiers while nuns had often acted as nurses. Nor was Nightingale the only woman who served as a nurse in the Crimea.
- Rather than the caring 'Lady with the Lamp' she is famed to be, Nightingale was more a tough-minded administrator.
- Despite her efforts, death rates continued to rise. Indeed, the death count at Nightingale's hospital – 4,000 over the winter of 1854–5 – was the highest of all the region's hospitals. Not until a Sanitary Commission was sent out in March 1855 was there an improvement. The Commission flushed out the sewers and improved ventilation.

The Royal Commission on the Health of the Army

On returning to Britain, Nightingale was determined to improve the health of troops. Through her efforts, a Royal Commission was appointed in 1857. Collecting evidence for the Commission, Nightingale realised that most of the soldiers at Scutari died as a result of poor hygiene and sanitation. Henceforward, she successfully promoted the overhaul of the army's health in general and the cause of improved sanitary conditions in particular.

The Nightingale Training School

In 1855, a public meeting to give recognition to Nightingale's work led to the establishment of a fund for the training of nurses. In 1860, the world's first secular nursing school – the Nightingale Training School – was set up at St Thomas' Hospital in London.

Nightingale's influence

- Nightingale inspired many women to devote their lives to nursing.
- A pioneer of modern nursing, she set an example of compassion, commitment to patient care and diligent administration.

Mary Seacole

Mary Seacole was the daughter of a Scottish army officer and a Jamaican woman. Taught herbal remedies by her mother, she helped to treat cholera victims in Jamaica and Panama in the 1840s and 1850s. Hearing of the poor medical provision for British soldiers, she applied to the War Office, hoping to be sent as an assistant to the Crimea – without success.

Borrowing money, she went out to Turkey. When Nightingale declined her offer of help, she sailed to Balaclava. Building a 'hotel' from salvaged materials, she nursed sick soldiers. Nightingale was ambivalent about Seacole, writing that 'she was very kind to the men...and did some good – and made many more drunk'. Russell in *The Times* was more complimentary, writing that she was a 'warm and successful physician, who doctors and cures all manner of men with extraordinary success'. Seacole is praised today for her achievements in overcoming the racial and gender prejudices of Victorian society.

Qualify your judgement

Below is a sample exam question with the accompanying source.

> Assess the value of Source 1 as evidence for a historian investigating the situation in the military hospitals at Scutari in November 1854 and for revealing the work of Florence Nightingale. Explain your answer, using the source, the information given about its origin, and your own knowledge about the historical context.

Having read the question and source, circle the judgement that best describes the value of the source and explain why it is the best.

1 Source 1 is valuable to a historian because it provides details of the conditions in Britain's military hospitals in November 1854.

2 Source 1 is not very valuable because it actually says very little about the situation in the military hospitals.

3 Source 1 is particularly valuable because it reveals some of Florence Nightingale's concerns – or at least the concerns she was prepared to reveal to the Secretary at War – in November 1854.

SOURCE 1

This was a letter, written by Florence Nightingale from the Barracks Hospital at Scutari on 25 November 1854. She was writing – in a private capacity – to Secretary at War Sidney Herbert. He was a personal friend and had officially supported her mission to the Black Sea. She had arrived at Scutari on 4 November with a team of 38 nurses.

1 It appears that, in these hospitals, the purveyor considers washing both of linen and of the men as 'minor detail' and during the three weeks we have been here, though our remonstrances have been treated with perfect civility, yet no washing whatever has been performed for the men, either of body linen or of bed linen, except by ourselves and a few wives of the wounded... The dirty shirts were collected yesterday for the first time, and on Monday *it is said* that they are to be washed, and we are organising a little washing establishment of our own, for the bandages etc. When we came here there was neither basin, towel, nor soap in the wards, nor any means of personal cleanliness for the wounded except the following: Thirty were bathed every night by Dr McGrigor's orders in slipper baths but this does not do more than include a washing once in eighty days for 2300 men. The consequences of all this are fever, cholera, gangrene, lice, bugs, fleas – and maybe erysipelas [an inflammatory disease, generally in the face] – from the using of one sponge among many wards. And even the slipper bathing does not apply to the General Hospital.

2 The fault here is *not* with the medical officers but in the separation of the department which affords every necessary supply, except medicines to them, and in the insufficient supply of minor officers in the Purveying Department under Mr Wreford, the purveyor general, as well as in the inevitable delay in obtaining supplies, occasioned by the existence of one single interpreter only, who is generally seen booted.

3 Your name is also continually used as a bugbear – they make a deity of cheapness and the secretary at war is synonymous here with Jupiter [The chief Roman God]... The cheese-parring system is here identified with you by the officers who carry it out. It is in vain to tell the purveyors that they will get no 'kudos' by this at home.

(From *Vol 14 The Collected Works of Florence Nightingale*, edited by Lynn McDonald, Wilfrid Laurier University Press, 2010)

Changing attitudes in Britain to the Crimean War

The impact of the press

While the Crimean War had a minimal impact on civilian life, war-reporting influenced British attitudes significantly.

Newspaper coverage

Newspaper coverage of the war, aided by the electric telegraph, ensured that the public was able to read about the reality of warfare with immediacy for the first time. Newspaper costs were falling thanks to new technology and the elimination of various duties. However, newspapers remained too expensive for most people, many of whom were still unable to read.

William Howard Russell

The most influential war reporter was **William Howard Russell** of *The Times*. He was present at the battle of Alma and sent extensive reports on the siege of Sebastopol. Raglan and his senior officers proved uncooperative, but Russell gained the respect and the trust of junior officers and ordinary troops. His reports highlighted the dreadful conditions experienced by soldiers, the ineffective treatment of the wounded and the mismanagement of supplies. While praising the bravery of British troops and initially avoiding criticism of Raglan, Russell asked awkward questions and, when he saw problems, he wrote about them. Russell's reportage was used by critics of the government and were a factor in bringing down the administration of the British Prime Minster, Lord Aberdeen, in January 1855.

Roger Fenton

Roger Fenton went to the Crimea in 1855 as the first official war photographer. The government hoped his photographs might counteract the (perceived) anti-war reporting of Russell and *The Times*. Given the primitive photographic technology, he was unable to take action shots. Thus, most of his photographs were posed pictures of men, mostly officers, or landscape images, including battlefields and cemeteries. His prints were displayed in London and also published in book-form. Newspapers at the time lacked the technology to print photographs; however, the *Illustrated London News* sent artists to the Crimea. Their sketches were converted into engravings for the paper.

Press attacks on Raglan

The army's plight in December 1854 stirred John Delane, *The Times'* editor, to criticise Raglan and the army's aristocratic leadership for incompetence. Raglan considered the attacks on him as unworthy of response, but was concerned that newspaper reporting might give the Russians useful information. Despite this, he did not attempt to get rid of the correspondents. The government also decided not to impose press censorship, fearing that, if it did so, it would be criticised for trying to hide its responsibility for the situation in the Crimea.

Palmerston

In January 1855, a motion to set up a committee to inquire into the conduct of the war was carried by 305 votes to 148. Prime Minister Lord Aberdeen resigned and was replaced by **Lord Palmerston**. Palmerston, popular with the public, benefited from the fact that much had already been done to remedy matters. His seemingly energetic administration made only modest changes to the war effort.

Administrative and military reform

As criticisms of military mismanagement grew, there were demands for military and government reform. Perceived blunders by the army's aristocratic leadership may have helped stimulate a new assertiveness in the middle classes. After 1856, governments introduced reforms which led to merit-based promotion in the Civil Service and British Army. However, the landed classes continued to maintain their grip on the army. The system of purchase of commissions did not end until Cardwell's reforms in 1871 (see page 70).

Complete the paragraph a

Below are a sample exam-style question and a paragraph written in answer to this question. The paragraph contains a point and specific examples, but lacks a concluding explanatory link back to the question. Complete the paragraph, adding this link in the space provided.

To what extent did the press influence public opinion on the Crimean War in the years 1854–6?

The Crimean War revealed the power of the press. Newspaper coverage of the war, aided by the electric telegraph, ensured that the public was able to read about the reality of warfare with immediacy for the first time. Thanks to new technology and the abolition of various taxes, the cost of newspapers was falling. That said, newspapers remained too expensive for most of the population.

_____

_____

Spectrum of significanc

Below are a sample exam-style question and a list of general points which could be used to answer the question. Use your own knowledge and the information in this section to reach a judgement about the importance of these general points to the question posed. Write numbers on the spectrum below to indicate their relative importance. Having done this, write a brief justification of your placement, explaining why some of these factors are more important than others. The resulting diagram could form the basis of an essay plan.

How far did the Crimean War impact on British life in the years 1854–6?

Less important ←——————————————————————→ More important

1 The Crimean War was a limited war from Britain's perspective.

2 The Crimean War revealed the power of the press.

3 William Howard Russell was an influential reporter.

4 The press helped bring about the fall of Lord Aberdeen.

5 Robert Fenton became the first official war photographer.

6 The war resulted in Civil Service reforms.

7 The war had only a limited impact on the British economy.

8 Paying for the war was not a serious problem.

Exam focus

Below is a sample essay. Read it and the comments around it.

To what extent did Florence Nightingale deserve her heroic reputation as a nurse during the Crimean War in the years 1854–6?

Florence Nightingale became a national heroine for her work with sick and wounded soldiers during the Crimean War. She was, until recently, seen as the only female nurse tending Crimean soldiers, and it was also assumed that she massively reduced the death rate in the Scutari hospital where she worked. Unfortunately (for Nightingale's reputation) the truth is rather different. She was by no means the only female nurse. Nor should her success at Scutari be exaggerated. According to historian Hugh Small, she effectively presided over a 'death camp'. While she helped her patients to die in greater comfort, she did not save their lives. Nevertheless, this essay will claim that Nightingale most definitely did – and does – deserve her heroic reputation.

During the Crimean War, Russian women cared for Russian sick and wounded, French nuns tended French soldiers and Irish nuns aided the British Army. Mary Stanley took a group of nurses to work at the hospital at Koulali, while Mary Seacole built a 'hotel' from salvaged materials – from which she served provisions and nursed sick soldiers. Seacole, the daughter of a Scottish army officer and a Jamaican woman, is now almost as famous as Nightingale. The work of Seacole, Stanley and the rest did not receive the same acclaim as that of Nightingale at the time however. Nor was it as important after 1856.

In mid-nineteenth-century Britain, women of a wealthy background did not become nurses, however, convinced she was doing God's work, Nightingale devoted her life to nursing. Despite her family's misgivings, Nightingale's father gave her a large income which allowed her to pursue her profession. When news of the appalling hospital conditions in the Crimea reached Britain, Nightingale volunteered to go out to help. Sidney Herbert, Secretary of State for War in 1854 and a personal friend of Nightingale's, authorised her mission. On 21 October 1854, Nightingale and 38 volunteer female nurses set out for the Black Sea. On their arrival at Selimiye Barracks in Scutari, the nurses found sick and wounded soldiers being badly cared for by overworked medical staff – all male. Medicines were in short supply and hygiene was neglected. The army's chief medical officers were deeply prejudiced against women's involvement in medicine but, despite this, Nightingale quickly set about improving matters.

Initially, Nightingale and her team were only allowed to undertake menial duties, however conditions in the Crimea worsed over the winter of 1854–5 and the number of hospitalised soldiers increased. Medical authorities needed all the help they could get and Nightingale's influence grew accordingly. £30,000 had been raised in Britain to help the soldiers, a fund which Nightingale oversaw and used to purchase badly needed necessities. She worked energetically to ensure that wards were cleaned, fresh bed linen was available and special diets were prepared. In many respects, rather than the caring 'Lady with the Lamp', Nightingale was an efficient team manager and a tough-minded administrator. Nightingale's considerable publicity ensured that the British public provided much needed funds to help care for the injured soldiers.

This is a confident and well-informed introduction that is very much linked to the set question and also sets out the course of the essay. The small quote adds weight to what is written.

This paragraph examines quite succinctly the point raised in the introduction about the fact that Nightingale was by no means the only pioneer. It shows detailed knowledge of names and events and the last sentence links back to the question.

Another excellent, well-written paragraph which continues to focus on the set question. The last sentence is an important one.

This is a concise paragraph with a clear analytical link to the question. It is full of relevant detail and the last sentence is again effective.

Despite the unstinting efforts of Nightingale and her team, death rates at Scutari rose rather than fell. Indeed, at 52 per cent, the death count at Nightingale's hospital was higher than all other hospitals in the region. Over the winter of 1854–5, some 4,000 soldiers died at Scutari. But, in fairness to Nightingale, at this stage she had no better understanding of the hazards of polluted water, lack of ventilation and poor hygiene than army doctors. Not until a government Sanitary Commission arrived in March 1855 was there a marked improvement. The Commission flushed out the sewers and improved the hospital's ventilation. It should be said, however, that Nightingale's work – and the publicity it received – was a factor in the Sanitary Commission's involvement in the Black Sea hospitals.

> This is a meaty, important paragraph. It does its best to defend Nightingale's reputation from pretty damning statistics. It just about succeeds. It should be said the paragraph is well-informed throughout.

After her return to Britain, Nightingale was determined to improve the health of British troops. Through her efforts a Royal Commission on the Health of the Army was appointed in 1857. Whilst collecting evidence for the Commission, Nightingale realised that most soldiers died as a result of poor hygiene and sanitation. Henceforward, she energetically promoted the thorough overhaul of the health of the army in general and the cause of improved sanitary conditions in particular. Shrewd and forceful, she manipulated her fame to masterly effect. As a result of the Royal Commission's findings and Nightingale's pressure, sanitation, diet and leisure facilities in army barracks and military hospitals were improved. An Army Medical School was established and the health of soldiers in India was dramatically improved. Nightingale also had a considerable impact on hospital design in Britain and across Europe, and set up the Nightingale Training School at St Thomas's Hospital. Her 1859 book, Notes on Nursing, was the first of its kind.

> This detailed paragraph, albeit out of the time range, includes information which is important to Nightingale's later reputation (itself built on the reputation she had gained in the Crimean War).

Thus, Nightingale deserved the plaudits she received during the Crimean War. Her work was important at the time – and for many years thereafter. Her achievements are all the more impressive when considered against the background of social restraints on women in Victorian Britain. Her contemporary Mary Seacole had to overcome both gender stereotyping and racial prejudice but, however notable Seacole's achievements were, her actual influence on nursing was minimal when compared with that of Nightingale. A national – indeed international – icon, Nightingale inspired tens of thousands of women to devote their lives to nursing. The pioneer of modern nursing, her work in the Crimean War set an example of compassion, commitment to patient care and diligent, thoughtful hospital administration.

> The conclusion pulls together the argument that was initiated in the introduction and developed throughout the essay. It presents a thoroughly consistent argument and ends with a fine last sentence.

This is a Level 5 essay due to the fact that it engages with the question and has a clear, balanced and carefully reasoned argument that is sustained throughout. The answer is very well written and covers most of the key areas, of which it shows excellent understanding.

Reverse engineering

The best essays are based on careful plans. Read the essay and the comments and try to work out the general points of the plan used to write the essay. Once you have done this, note down the specific examples used to support each general point.

Facing the Boers in southern Africa, 1899–1900 REVISED ☐

The British Army in 1899

In 1899, Britain went to war against two **Boer** republics: the Transvaal and the Orange Free State.

In some respects, the British Army was well-prepared for war.
- Officers and men were experienced from a number of colonial wars, in which military leaders had responded well to scientific and technological innovation.
- Once war was declared, mobilisation went well, with the Admiralty quickly transporting men and supplies to southern Africa.

Nevertheless, there were problems:
- There was a shortage of ammunition.
- Several departments, for example the Medical Corps, were understaffed.
- Intelligence and staff work were inadequate.

The Boer Army in 1899

On paper, the Boer Army looked no match for the British:
- The Boers could put fewer than 60,000 men in the field.
- The Boer Army was essentially a civilian militia. When danger loomed, all adult male citizens in a district were expected to form a **commando**. Each man brought his own weapon and horse.

But the Boers should not have been underestimated:
- The First Boer War (1880–1) suggested that the Boers, excellent horsemen and hunters, were likely to be tough opponents.
- The Boers were armed with some of Europe's best weapons, including the powerful Mauser rifle.
- Boers believed that they were engaged in a life-and-death struggle to preserve their distinctive culture.
- Many Boers in the British territories of Cape Colony and Natal sympathised with the two Boer republics.

The significance of the sieges of Ladysmith, Mafeking and Kimberley

Sir George White, with 10,000 men from the Indian Army, arrived in Natal on 7 October 1899, in time to prevent the Boers marching unimpeded on Durban. Nevertheless, Boer forces initially outnumbered British forces in southern Africa: troops did not sail from Britain until 12 October.

Ladysmith, Mafeking and Kimberley

After the war's first battle at Dundee (20 October), White established a base at the garrison town of Ladysmith, which was soon surrounded by Boer forces. An attack on Boer positions was a disastrous failure and enabled the Boers to lay siege to the town.

Colonel Robert Baden-Powell, who had raised some 1,200 men was besieged in the town of Mafeking by 7,000 Boers.

In November, a force of 7,500 Boers laid siege to the diamond-mining town of Kimberley.

Attempts to relieve the sieges

General Sir Redvers Buller arrived in Cape Town on 31 October, followed on 18 November by the first contingent of the First Army Corps. This changed the balance of power in Britain's favour. Buller split his army into three detachments:
- General Lord Methuen, with 20,000 men, set out to relieve Kimberley and Mafeking.
- General Gatacre, with 3,000 men, headed towards Stormberg to secure the northern Cape.
- Buller led the main force, 30,000 men, to relieve Ladysmith.

Methuen won two small but costly victories at Belmont (23 November) and at Graspan (25 November), but was defeated at the Modder River (28 November).

The impact of Black Week, December 1899

In 'Black Week' (10–15 December 1899), British forces suffered a series of defeats:
- On 10 December, Gatacre lost over 700 soldiers trying to take Stormberg.
- On 11 December, Methuen suffered 900 casualties at Magersfontein. He failed to relieve Kimberley.
- On 15 December, Buller, with 21,000 men, tried to cross the Tugela River at Colenso. Facing 8,000 Boers, Buller suffered nearly 1,400 casualties. Eight Boers died.

The Boers, fighting on the defensive, had the advantage of prepared positions, and were armed with smokeless, **magazine rifles** which could kill at 2,000 yards.

Spot the mistake

Below are a sample exam-style question and an introductory paragraph written in answer to this question. Why does this paragraph not get into Level 4? Once you have identified the mistake, rewrite the paragraph so that it displays the qualities of Level 4. The mark scheme on pages 94–5 will help you.

To what extent was the British Army prepared for war in 1899?

> The British Army was small in 1899. Not much had been done to boost numbers or to bring the army up to a higher level of professionalism. The government had not been keen to spend money on the army.

 Develop the detail

Below are a sample exam-style question and a paragraph written in answer to this question. The paragraph contains a limited amount of detail. Annotate the paragraph to add additional detail to the answer.

To what extent were British failures in the Boer War in 1899 due to poor leadership?

> The Boer Army should not have been underestimated. The First Boer War suggested that the Boers were likely to be tough opponents. Many Boers in Cape Colony and Natal sympathised with the Transvaal and the Orange Free State.

Turning the tide: British victories, 1900

The War in 1900

After his defeat at Colenso, Buller was replaced as commander by **Lord Roberts**, hero of the 1880 Afghan War. **Lord Kitchener**, hero of the 1898 Sudan campaign, was appointed Roberts' chief of staff.

British recruitment

Learning of the defeats, Britons rushed to join the army. By January 1900, 180,000 troops, the largest force Britain had ever sent overseas, were in southern Africa. Some 30,000 men from British-controlled southern Africa came forward as volunteers, as did men from Australia, Canada and New Zealand in a display of imperial solidarity.

Lord Roberts

Roberts arrived at the Cape in January 1900. He issued new tactical guidelines, insisting on careful reconnaissance before an attack, the avoidance of frontal attacks in mass formations and more use of cover. Leaving Buller in command in Natal, Roberts massed his main force near the Orange River and prepared to make an outflanking move designed to relieve Kimberley and then take Bloemfontein. Kitchener improvised a transport system of wagons, unshackling British troops from dependence on railway lines.

Spion Kop

Buller, reinforced, made another bid to relieve Ladysmith. British forces crossed the Tugela west of Colenso but then faced a Boer defensive position centred on a hill known as Spion Kop. British troops, which captured the summit on 24 January, found themselves overlooked by Boer gun emplacements on surrounding hills. The result was 1,350 casualties and a retreat back across the Tugela.

The relief of Kimberley, Ladysmith and Mafeking

- Roberts and Kitchener launched their offensive on 10 February, intending to outflank the Boers defending Magersfontein. To ensure greater mobility, they doubled the number of their mounted infantry. On 15 February, British cavalry relieved Kimberley. On 28 February, Roberts forced the surrender of a 4,000 Boer army at Paardeberg.
- On 26 February, Buller succeeded in crossing the Tugela and defeating the Boers. Ladysmith was finally relieved.
- Roberts now advanced into the Orange Free State, putting the Boers to flight at Poplar Grove (7 March) and capturing Bloemfontein (13 March). Roberts was then forced to delay for six weeks because:
  - his army was short of supplies
  - almost 1,000 troops died in an outbreak of typhoid.
- Despite these problems, Roberts was able to send a small force towards Mafeking, which was relieved on 17 May after a 217-day siege, provoking huge celebrations in Britain. Its defender, Baden-Powell, became a national hero – with good cause. He had tied down 7,000 Boers, almost a fifth of their forces, at a crucial period.

In May, Roberts continued his advance. Given the overwhelming superiority of British numbers, the Boers could only retreat. On 28 May, the Orange Free State was annexed. Meeting little resistance, Roberts captured Johannesburg (31 May) and Pretoria (5 June). President Kruger of the Transvaal, and what remained of his government, retreated eastwards. Roberts advanced down the railway line leading to **Portuguese East Africa**, breaking the Boers' defensive position at Bergendal on 26 August. Kruger fled to Europe. The remains of the Boer Army crossed into the Transvaal high **veldt**.

It seemed the war was over. In September 1900, the Transvaal was formally annexed. Many British troops returned home to a heroes' welcome. In November, after handing over to Kitchener, Roberts set sail for England, where he became Commander-in-Chief and was voted £100,000 by Parliament.

Support or challenge?

Below is a sample exam-style question which asks how far you agree with a specific statement. Below this is a series of general statements which are relevant to the question. Using your own knowledge and the information on the opposite page, decide whether these statements support or challenge the statement in the question and tick the appropriate box.

'Good leadership explains British success in the Boer War in 1900.' How far do you agree with this view?

	Support	Challenge
Britain sent large numbers of troops to South Africa.		
Lord Roberts replaced Buller as commander-in-chief.		
The Boers wasted their efforts in sieges.		
British forces took Spion Kop.		
Roberts introduced new tactical guidelines.		
Roberts and Kitchener increased the number of their mounted infantry.		
By May 1900, Britain had an overwhelming superiority of forces.		
British forces relieved Mafeking in May 1900.		
Roberts continued to press the Boers throughout the summer.		
Roberts adopted a scorched earth policy.		

Simple essay style

Below is a sample exam-style question. Use your own knowledge and the information on the opposite page to produce a plan for this question. Choose four general points and provide three pieces of specific information to support each general point. Once you have planned the essay, write the introduction and conclusion for the essay. The introduction should list the points to be discussed in the essay. The conclusion should summarise the key points and justify which point was the most important.

To what extent do Britain's superior number of forces explain Lord Roberts' success in 1900?

The role of British commanders in achieving victory

General Sir Redvers Buller

Buller took command of forces in South Africa in October 1899. He intended to go on the offensive against the Boers with a direct assault on Pretoria, capital of the Transvaal, but was forced to abandon this strategy in order to relieve the besieged towns. Buller moved towards Ladysmith, but suffered a significant defeat by Boer forces at Colenso.

Buller had advised White to surrender Ladysmith, advice that was criticised in Britain, and led (in part) to his replacement by Roberts. Buller was given a hero's welcome on his return to Britain late in 1900, but many British newspapers were critical of his leadership and, in 1901, he was strongly attacked by the journalist Leo Amery. Buller responded to Amery's criticisms in a speech. The government accused him of breaching military discipline and he was summarily dismissed.

Field Marshal Roberts

Roberts took command of the South African armies in January 1900. He devised a two-pronged attack on the Boers:
- to relieve the besieged towns
- to launch direct attacks on the Boer territories of the Orange Free State and the Transvaal.

In February 1900, British forces relieved Kimberley and Ladysmith, while Mafeking was taken in May.

Roberts took Bloemfontein, capital of the Orange Free State, in March, and captured Pretoria in May.

Boer fighters maintained their resistance throughout the summer, but their opposition disintegrated when their political leaders fled abroad and the British annexed their territories.

Field Marshal Kitchener

Kitchener was appointed Commander-in-Chief in November 1900 and oversaw the last months of the war. His actions were important in ensuring the final defeat of the Boers:

- He continued Roberts' scorched earth policy, with the burning of farms and homesteads and the destruction of food and livestock.
- Concentration camps were set up for Boer families who had been forced to quit their homes. The camps would also prevent civilians assisting the commandos.
- In humanitarian terms the concentration camp policy was disastrous. Inadequate food, poor hygiene and sanitation and shortage of medical facilities led to diseases such as measles, typhoid and dysentery. Over 20,000 Boer women and children died in the 45 camps; one in four of the inmates. Tens of thousands of black Africans were also forcibly removed and placed in separate camps. Over 12,000 black inmates probably died.
- The high death rate in the camps was the result of incompetence, not a deliberate policy of extermination. Kitchener argued that leaving Boer families on the ransacked veldt would have been even crueller.
- Kitchener, endeavouring to restrict the movement of Boer raiders, built 8,000 fortified blockhouses, each housing six to eight soldiers. The blockhouses were eventually linked with barbed wire fences, stretching over 4,000 miles and parcelling the veldt into small areas. British troops conducted 'sweeps' across these areas in an attempt to trap the enemy. Mounted raiding columns supported the larger sweeper columns. British forces deployed the latest technology, maintaining communications through the telephone and telegraph cable.

Kitchener's tactics of containment and harassment worked. By early 1902, it was obvious, even to Boer 'bitter-enders' that further resistance was futile. The war ended with the Treaty of Vereeniging (May 1902). 22,000 British soldiers had died – 7,792 in battle, the rest through disease. 7,000 Boer soldiers died. The war, which required the services of 450,000 British and colonial troops, cost taxpayers £217 million.

Mind map

Use the information on the opposite page to add detail to the mind map below. This information should help you understand the main events of the Boer War from 1900–2.

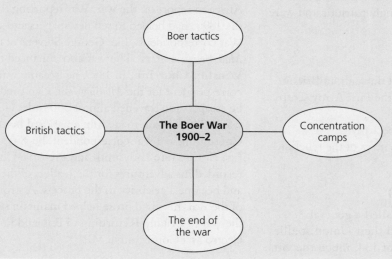

 Introducing an argument

Below are a sample exam-style question, a list of key points to be made in the essay and a simple introduction and conclusion for the essay. Read the question, the plan and the introduction and conclusion. Rewrite the introduction and the conclusion in order to develop an argument.

'Kitchener showed great skill in southern Africa in the years 1900–2.' Explain why you agree or disagree with this view.

Key points
- Boer tactics 1900–2
- British tactics 1900–2
- Concentration camps
- The end of the war

Introduction

In November 1900, Kitchener was appointed to command the British Army in southern Africa. He proved himself to be a capable leader, developing tactics which ultimately defeated the hard-line Boer guerrillas.

Conclusion

In May 1902, Boer commandos accepted defeat. Kitchener's tactics of containment and harassment had been generally successful, with the exception of his concentration camp policy in 1900–1.

The impact of the Boer War on attitudes in Britain

Popular support for the war

Most MPs supported the war in 1899. In all likelihood, so did most Britons. Most were strongly patriotic and were proud of the British Empire.

Khaki fever

In 1899–1900, 'khaki fever' raged throughout Britain.
- Half a million people cheered the First Army Corps as it left Southampton.
- Men rushed to volunteer for the army.
- Passionate celebrations greeted news of the relief of Mafeking.

The 'khaki election', 1900

In September 1900, Salisbury called a general election. The Conservatives and their Unionist allies were returned with a majority of 134, much the same as in 1895.

Historians struggle to make sense of the 'khaki election'. In some constituencies, the election was dominated by the war. Elsewhere the war took second place to other issues. Arguably, the election results reflected the disorganisation of the Liberal opposition rather than a vote in support of the war.

The press and the war

The press, as well as encouraging support for both the imperial idea and the war, probably reflected the views of the general public. By the 1890s, more Britons could afford to buy daily newspapers, the costs of which were falling as a result of technical improvements and advertising revenue. Some 150 daily papers catered for the tastes of an expanding reading public and the dailies were supplemented by a plethora of weekly papers and monthly periodicals.

The *Daily Mail*

In 1896, Alfred Harmsworth launched the *Daily Mail*, selling his paper for a halfpenny when most established papers cost a penny. By 1900, the *Mail* had a circulation of nearly one million, far more than its rivals. The paper was fiercely imperialist, and a vigorous supporter of the war.

War correspondents

Many newspapers sent war correspondents to southern Africa to report on the war. War reporting throughout the 1890s had helped to sell newspapers and some Boer War correspondents, like George Stevens of the *Daily Mail*, became 'stars'. The war also enhanced the career of **Winston Churchill**. In 1899, he became war correspondent for the *Morning Post*. Captured by Boers, he escaped and travelled almost 300 miles (480 km) to safety. This exploit made him a national hero. Continuing as a war correspondent, he was among the first Britons into Ladysmith and Pretoria. Churchill recorded his adventures for the readers of the *Morning Post* and became a celebrity in the process. A strong supporter of the war, his vivid prose helped maintain support for the war in Britain. Returning to England in 1900, he was elected as a Conservative MP.

War correspondents exercised huge political influence through their reporting of the news and their control over its dissemination. Image could be as potent as reality, particularly when it came to military reputations. General Buller's contempt for the press and his heavy-handed methods of censorship harmed him dearly. Unable to present his own side of the story, he was widely depicted by journalists as a buffoon. Roberts, by contrast, went out of his way to butter up the correspondents. He also took care to keep them away from unpleasant scenes such as the typhoid epidemic.

The impact of other media

- The war was captured through photographs. Troops, as well as journalists, had access to cartridge film first used in the Pocket and Bullet Kodaks of 1896, supplemented from 1900 by the cheap Brownie camera.
- As a result of the **bioscope**, invented in 1895, audiences could see moving pictures from southern Africa. However 'staged' much of the footage was, it gave the war a sharper immediacy.

! Complete the paragraph a

Below are a sample exam-style question and a paragraph written in answer to this question. The paragraph contains a point and a concluding explanatory link back to the question, but lacks examples. Complete the paragraph, adding examples in the space provided.

To what extent did the British press impact on the Boer War in the years 1899–1902?

By 1899, the press had considerable power. Most Britons could now afford to buy daily newspapers.

_____

_____

The press was the main medium for politicians to put their views to the people and for people to keep themselves informed.

! Developing an argument

Below are a sample exam-style question, a list of key points to be made in the essay and a paragraph from the essay. Read the question, the plan and the sample paragraph. Rewrite the paragraph in order to develop an argument. Your paragraph should explain why the factor discussed in the paragraph is linked to the question.

'In many ways, war correspondents had greater power than generals.' How far do you agree with this statement about the Boer War in the years 1899–1902?

Key points
- The power of the press
- The *Daily Mail*
- War correspondents
- The impact of newspapers on the Boer War

Sample paragraph

Many newspapers sent war correspondents to southern Africa to report on the war at first hand. War reporting throughout the 1890s had been popular with the public and had helped to sell newspapers. Some Boer War correspondents like George Stevens of the Daily Mail and Winston Churchill of the Morning Post became 'stars'. War correspondents exercised enormous influence through their access to news and their control over its dissemination. Image could be as potent as reality, particularly when it came to military reputations.

Opposition to the war

A sizeable minority of the population vehemently opposed the war from the start. They were backed by newspapers like the *Manchester Guardian* and assorted socialist journals.

Opposition to imperialism

Not all Britons supported imperialism:
- Some writers and politicians insisted that imperial ambitions distracted attention from domestic social problems.
- Critics of imperialism saw greed as the motivating force in overseas expansion.
- Imperial issues had split the Liberal Party between Liberal Imperialists and Radical Liberals.

Radical Liberal opposition to the war

The Radical Liberals' case was stated, at its simplest, in a resolution drafted by **Lloyd George** in 1900. The resolution denounced the war as 'a crime and a blunder, committed at the instigation of irresponsible capitalists'.

Labour and the trade unions

Organised labour took a cautious approach. The Trades Union Congress officially maintained a position of neutrality, partly because the leadership did not wish to pick a quarrel with those trade unionists who had rushed to join the army. Members of the fledgling Labour Party tended to believe that the conflict was a capitalist war. But some Labour leaders announced that in a national emergency they were Britons first and socialists second.

Irish Nationalist opposition

The war's most outspoken opponents were the Irish Nationalists who regarded the Boers as fellow-victims of imperialist aggression.

The role of Emily Hobhouse

Emily Hobhouse was a British welfare campaigner, pacifist and humanitarian who played a significant role in highlighting the appalling conditions in South Africa's concentration camps, forcing the government to take action.

Hobhouse's work in England, 1899–1900

In 1899, Hobhouse became secretary to the South African Conciliation Committee, which campaigned against the South African war. In 1900 she set up a fund to provide aid and supplies for Boer families. The fund was generously supported by the Quakers, but it received very few contributions from the British public.

Hobhouse in South Africa, 1900

Hobhouse landed in South Africa in December 1900. Over the next few months she investigated conditions at Port Elizabeth and Bloemfontein, along with several other camps in the heart of the country. She managed to arrange supplies for some camps, but military authorities obstructed her work at every turn.

Hobhouse's report to the government, June 1901

On her return to England, Hobhouse submitted a report to the government which provided in great detail the conditions which she had seen in South Africa:
- Families were usually accommodated in tents which were overcrowded and provided little protection from the weather.
- Food rations were scarce and inadequate. Most children were undernourished, which meant that childhood diseases such as measles were often fatal.
- Water was in short supply and insanitary conditions led to frequent and widespread outbreaks of typhoid.
- Hobhouse called for the end of the scorched earth policy and the forcible relocation of families into the camps.

The report was taken up by Lloyd George and other Radical Liberals. Their leader, Campbell-Bannerman, attacked 'the methods of barbarism' occurring in South Africa.

The Fawcett Commission

The government's response was to send a commission to South Africa, led by Millicent Fawcett, to investigate the camps. The commission confirmed every one of Hobhouse's findings. It recommended a long list of measures, including the need for increased rations and more nurses. Civil authorities took over the running of the camps and the death rate dropped considerably.

In December 1901, Kitchener instructed his commanders not to bring Boer families in to the camps when they 'cleared' the country. This was a shrewd move. While seeming to appease his critics, it also handicapped the guerrillas, who now had to care for their families.

! Complete the paragraph   a

Below are a sample exam-style question and a paragraph written in answer to this question. The paragraph contains a point and a concluding explanatory link back to the question, but lacks examples. Complete the paragraph, adding examples in the space provided.

To what extent was the British public opposed to the Boer War?

> There is no doubt that a sizeable minority of the population opposed the war from the start.
>
> _____
>
> _____

> Thus, from the outbreak of war in October 1899 a number of influential anti-war groups campaigned against the war.

⭥ Support or challenge?

Below is a sample exam-style question which asks how far you agree with a specific statement. Below this is a series of general statements which are relevant to the question. Using your own knowledge and the information on the opposite page, decide whether these statements support or challenge the statement in the question and tick the appropriate box.

'The Boer War led to a decline in imperial sentiment.' How far do you agree with this statement?

	Support	Challenge
After 1902, imperialism became synonymous with 'methods of barbarism'.		
Popular newspapers continued to be stridently imperialistic.		
Britons continued to be bombarded with imperial imagery.		
The Liberal Party was in power from 1905–1914.		
Joseph Chamberlain's tariff reform proposals proved unpopular.		
British patriotism remained strong.		
Many Britons associated imperialism with capitalism.		
Many Britons emigrated to Canada, New Zealand and Australia after 1902.		

Exam focus

Below are a sample source, question and answer to the question. Read the source. Then read the answer and the comments around it.

Assess the value of Source 1 for revealing information about the military situation in southern Africa in January 1901 and as evidence for Emily Hobhouse's motivation for going to southern Africa.

SOURCE 1

This source is part of a letter written by Miss Emily Hobhouse to the Manchester Guardian *newspaper. Emily Hobhouse went to South Africa in December 1900 to investigate conditions in the British concentration camps. She went on behalf of the South African Women and Children's Distress Fund. While she was in South Africa, she wrote a series of letters which were printed in the* Manchester Guardian.

January 22 1901

I had a splendid truck given me at Capetown through the kind cooperation of Sir Alfred Milner – a large double-covered one, capable of holding 12 tons. I took £200 worth of groceries, besides all the bales of clothing I could muster. The truck left Capetown the day before myself, was hitched on to my train at De Aar, and so arrived when I did..... Going through the Karoo it was very hot, and the second day there were horrible duststorms, varied by thunderstorms...From Colesberg on it was a desolate outlook. The land seemed dead and silent as far as the eye could reach, absolutely without life, only carcasses of horses, mules and cattle with a sort of acute anguish on their look, and bleached bones and refuse...I saw a few burnt farms, but those unburnt seemed still and lifeless also, and no work is going on in the fields. Really, the line the whole way up is a string of Tommies, yawning at their posts....But I must pass on to tell you about the Women's Camp, which, after all, is the central point of interest.

January 26 1901

The Bloemfontein Camp

The exile camp here is a good two miles from the town, dumped down on the southern slope of a kopje [hill], right out on to the bare brown veld, not a vestige of a tree in any direction, nor shade of any description. It was about four o'clock of a scorching afternoon when I set foot in the camp, and I can't tell you what I felt like so I won't try.

I began by finding a woman whose sister I had met in Capetown. It is such a puzzle to find your way in a village of bell tents, no streets or names or numbers. There are nearly 2000 people in this one camp, of which some few are men – they call them 'hands up men' – and over 900 children. Imagine the heat outside the tents and the suffocation inside! We sat on their khaki blankets, rolled up, inside Mrs. B.'s tent and the sun blazed through the single canvas, and the flies lay thick and black on everything; no chair, no table, nor any room for such; only a deal box standing on its end, served as a wee pantry. In this tiny tent live Mrs. B.'s five children (three quite grown up) and a little Kaffir servant girl. Many tents have more occupants.

Mrs P. came in, and Mrs R. and others, and they told me their stories, and we cried together and even laughed together. On wet nights the water streams down through the canvas and comes flowing in, as it knows how to do in this country, under a flap of the tent and wets their blankets, as they lie on the ground. While we sat there a snake came in. They said it was a puff adder, very poisonous, so they all ran out and I attacked the creature with my parasol. I could not bear to think the thing should be at large in a community mostly sleeping on the ground. After a struggle I wounded it, and then a man came in with a mallet and finished it off.

The source, written in January 1901, provides a vivid account of some aspects of the military situation in southern Africa. Britain, nominally in control of both the Orange Free State and the Transvaal, was struggling to defeat the hard core of Boers – perhaps some 20,000 men – who refused to concede defeat. Most of these men had returned to their home districts where they could rely on local support and had personal knowledge of the terrain. Ordered to act against the British whenever possible, their tactics were to strike hard and fast, causing as much damage as possible, and then to withdraw and vanish before British reinforcements could arrive. The vast size of the republics made it difficult for the 250,000 British troops to control territory effectively. As soon as a British column left a district, British authority faded away.

> This introductory paragraph helps put the source in context. It shows good understanding of the situation in January 1901, but might have said more – or even something – about the source's value.

General Kitchener, who was now the military commander in southern Africa, adopted a variety of policies to deal with the Boer guerrillas. One policy was to burn farms thought to be giving support to the Boer commandos. This scorched earth strategy (which had begun under Lord Roberts) targeted everything that might give sustenance to Boer guerrillas. As British troops swept the countryside, they destroyed property and crops, salted fields and poisoned wells. Hobhouse saw evidence of this policy as she headed north. She describes the 'carcases of horses, mules and cattle', 'bleached bones' and 'burnt farms'. Hobhouse also makes reference to Kitchener's need to control the railway lines. These were vital to his supply lines and frequently came under Boer attack. Hobhouse writes that all the way along the railway line on which she was travelling there was 'a string of Tommies'. She implies that most were bored out of their minds.

> This paragraph begins with context and ends by linking that context to the source. This is good technique. The paragraph is well-informed and well-written.

Hobhouse's main evidence, however, is her description of the concentration camps, administered by the British Army. These had been set up as refugee camps for families who had been forced to quit their homes. While following naturally from the scorched earth policy, the moving of Boer women and children into camps was also intended to prevent civilians assisting the Boer guerrillas. In military terms, the concentration camp policy may have been a mistake. Although in the long run it perhaps undermined the Boers' will to resist, in the short term it freed them from responsibility for their families and thus had the opposite effect of that intended. Miss Hobhouse was not particularly concerned with military policy. Her main concern were the humanitarian issues arising from the concentration camp policy. Her description of the camp at Bloemfontein makes it abundantly clear that camp conditions were far from good. The camp, badly situated, on the bare veldt had more than 2,000 people, mainly but not entirely women and children, who were housed in bell tents. She describes one tent in which Mrs B lived with her five children and a black maid. (This was unusual: most black Africans were placed in separate camps.) The tents, which contained no furniture, were infested with flies. Nor did they keep out the sun's heat, heavy rain, or snakes – a hazard to people sleeping on the ground. In this particular extract, Hobhouse does not mention other – more serious – problems: inadequate food, bad hygiene and sanitation and shortage of medical facilities. These conditions were to lead to the spread of diseases such as measles, typhoid and dysentery to which Boer children were particularly vulnerable. Over 20,000 Boer women and children were to die in the forty-five camps, about one in four of the inmates.

> This paragraph is excellent on both background knowledge and paraphrasing of the source.

Hobhouse had gone out to South Africa to see for herself the conditions in the camps. Her main aim was to help the people in the camps. Her second was to make the British people aware of the conditions. Hobhouse's reports were printed in the Manchester Guardian, a newspaper which opposed the war. With her reports Hobhouse hoped to influence public opinion and cause enough of an outcry to either improve, or bring an end to, the camps. Hobhouse had opposed the Boer War from its outset. In October 1899, she became secretary of the woman's branch of the South African Conciliation Committee, an organisation committed to bringing about peace. She also founded the Distress Fund for South African Women and Children. In short, her reporting was unlikely to be unbiased.

Hobhouse's bias is not too apparent in this particular source extract. She does not condemn the military authorities (she did in other letters!) or the political authorities. Indeed, she thanks Sir Alfred Milner for his 'kind co-operation' in providing her with a splendid truck. As already stated, this particular source (unlike many others) does not mention the horrific death rates in many of the concentration camps. Indeed, she seems to report things essentially as they were. While she is clearly sympathetic to the plight of Mrs B and the other women in Bloemfontein camp, she does not overstate their suffering. She perhaps boasts a little when describing her encounter with the puff adder which she fought off with her parasol. But why not? The story was a good one and one likely to engage her readers.

Hobhouse's description of camp conditions in a report issued in June 1901 created an international outcry. German Chancellor von Bulow denounced Britain's treatment of the Boers as 'brutal and inhuman'. Liberal leader Henry Campbell-Bannerman now came off the fence and attacked the methods of 'barbarism' being used in southern Africa.

Hobhouse's reporting in Source 1 is typical of her general reporting. She wrote what she saw and generally did so in a fair and accurate manner. A government-appointed commission, headed by Millicent Fawcett (a government supporter), conducted its own tour of the concentration camps between August and December 1901. The commission's findings confirmed everything Hobhouse had said. This led to government action. Civil authorities took over the running of the camps and, by early 1902, the death rate for white inmates dropped to two per cent. But by then the damage had been done.

Source 1, therefore, is a most useful source for historians studying the military situation in January 1901 – particularly the concentration camp policy – and for studying Hobhouse's own motivation. While this source is not as damning as other letters and reports by Hobhouse, it gives a feel for the way she wrote. Yes, she had her own agenda – to help Boer women and children by exposing the conditions in the camps. But she did not overstate the situation in the camps. Her reporting, as in this source, was usually factual, fair and clear – as clear as her own motivation in going to southern Africa in the first place.

This paragraph deals with the second part of the question. It is very well-informed but does not altogether get to grips with the question. What exactly does the source show?

This is an excellent paragraph. It makes some trenchant points and links context and source to good effect.

This short paragraph does not really help the essay's cause. It's all context and makes no reference to the source. Even the context is not too relevant.

This paragraph makes one or two very valid points.

This is a pretty good conclusion. It makes some incisive points about the overall value of the source.

This is a Level 4 answer. It shows excellent knowledge of the historical context. This is used to reveal and discuss some aspects of the source's strengths and limitations. But the essay is generally weaker in terms of analysing the source, demonstrated by examining the evidence to make reasoned inferences.

Moving from a Level 4 to Level 5

The exam focus essay at the end of Section 1 (pages 18–21) provided a Level 5 essay. The essay here achieves a Level 4. Read both essays and the comments provided. Make a list of the additional features required to push a Level 4 source-based essay into Level 5.

4 Trench warfare on the Western Front, 1914–18

The British Army's readiness for war

The First World War began in August 1914. Britain was initially allied with France, Russia, Serbia and Belgium against Germany and Austria-Hungary. On 4 August 1914, Britain's regular army consisted of nearly 250,000 men. The part-time territorial force had some 270,000 men.

Lord Kitchener

On 5 August 1914, Lord Kitchener became Secretary of State for War. Virtually alone among British leaders, he forecast a three- or four-year long war and realised that Britain would have to put huge armies into the field. He set about planning accordingly, aiming to construct a series of 'New Armies'. Recruitment exceeded all expectations. Some 761,000 men joined the army in August and September.

High command

The British Expeditionary Force (BEF) was commanded by Sir John French who had fought in Egypt and South Africa. French, his staff at general headquarters (**GHQ**) and his divisional and corps commanders had little practice or training at their respective levels of command. Officer training had not prepared senior commanders very well for modern war. Most British generals were committed to taking the offensive.

Munition problems

The army was deficient in modern technology. In 1914:
- only two machine guns were available to each battalion
- the entire army had only 80 motor vehicles.

Worse still, in August 1914, barely 6,000 rifles and 30,000 rounds of shells a month were being produced. The War Office's decision to concentrate orders in the hands of government ordnance factories limited the industry's ability to respond to new demands.

From a war of movement to attrition

In 1914, in accordance with the Schlieffen Plan, 1.5 million German troops marched through Belgium, aiming to crush France.

Mons and Le Cateau

The 120,000-strong BEF was sent to Mauberge on the French left. On 23 August, 75,000 BEF troops checked the advance of 300,000 German troops at Mons. Whilst retreating, the BEF fought a costly rearguard action at Le Cateau (26 August), before continuing its withdrawal.

The Battle of the Marne

In September, a French army defeated the Germans at the Battle of the Marne, forcing the Germans to retreat to the River Aisne. The Germans dug in, and it was here that they first discovered that trenches with machine guns could stop attackers. They thus established the first section of the defensive earthwork of the Western Front.

The first Battle of Ypres

Both sides now tried to outflank each other by 'racing to the sea'. Dogged resistance from the BEF at Ypres ensured that the Allies retained control of crucial Channel ports.

Stalemate

By December, a line of trenches ran for over 475 miles from the Channel to Switzerland – a thin line by later standards, but solid enough to prevent a war of movement. British forces held about 35 miles of this line. The BEF, despite its small size, had fought well. The most serious problems had been at high command level. Sir John French had maintained only tenuous control at critical points.

Spectrum of significance

Below are a sample exam-style question and a list of general points which could be used to answer the question. Use your own knowledge and the information on the opposite page to reach a judgement about the importance of these general points to the question posed. Write numbers on the spectrum below to indicate their relative importance. Having done this, write a brief justification of your placement, explaining why some of these factors are more important than others. The resulting diagram could form the basis of an essay plan.

> 'Given their state of readiness, British military forces performed better than might have been expected in 1914.' How far do you agree with this statement?

←———→

Less important   Very important

1   The strength of the British Army in 1914

2   Lord Kitchener's role

3   Pals regiments

4   The shortage of army officers

5   The BEF's high command

6   Munitions problems

7   Naval readiness in 1914

8   The British Army in action in 1914

Develop the detail   **a**

Below are a sample exam-style question and a paragraph written in answer to this question. The paragraph contains a limited amount of detail. Annotate the paragraph to add additional detail to the answer.

> To what extent was the British Army well prepared for war by the end of 1914?

The British Army was woefully deficient in modern technology in August 1914. Each infantry battalion, for example, had only two machine guns. Worse still, the stock of munitions was grossly inadequate. The situation did not improve much during the first months of the war. Indiscriminate recruiting led to the enlistment of many skilled engineers who could not easily be replaced.

The need for military adjustment

Trying to break the stalemate

In 1915, the Western Front developed into a complex network of trenches, protected on both sides by barbed wire. Offensive actions by British forces to break the stalemate led to huge casualties:

- An unsuccessful British offensive at Neuve Chapelle (10–13 March) led to 13,000 British casualties.
- On 22 April, the Germans launched an offensive (the second Battle of Ypres) using chlorine gas. British troops held firm but suffered 60,000 casualties.
- British attacks at Aubers Ridge and Festubert in May failed. The British suffered 16,500 casualties.

Since traditional methods of warfare were unsuccessful, the British government attempted to find solutions to the deadlock with new techniques of warfare and with new technology.

The machine gun

In 1884, Hiram Maxim invented the first fully automatic machine gun, which was adopted by every major power. The Maxim machine gun was very heavy and required a gun crew of at least four men. Early models tended to overheat and jam, but later models became more efficient as the war progressed. Germany saw its value as a weapon of defence: by 1914 the German Army had deployed 12,000 guns, while Britain had just a few hundred. Mass infantry attacks on German defensive positions usually ended in total failure.

British forces adopted the Vickers machine gun and, from 1915, relied on the lighter and more reliable American Lewis gun.

Chlorine gas

German forces were the first to engage in gas attacks, at Ypres in 1915. The British responded later that year, but the wind blew the gas back onto its own troops. By 1916, Britain had developed the gas shell, which increased the range of attacks. Chlorine gas was lethal but inefficient and Britain found that phosgene was a more effective form of gas, killing troops within 48 hours.

Despite its fearsome reputation, gas was not an effective weapon. Although over one million men were gassed during the war, in total only 91,000 men were killed.

The tank

Tanks were first used by British forces at the Somme in 1916, when fifty machines were sent against German lines. Most broke down or got bogged down in the muddy ground. Despite several modifications in 1917 and 1918, the mechanical unreliability of tanks meant that they never achieved a decisive breakthrough against German forces.

Fuze 106

Barbed wire was an effective defensive weapon used by both sides: existing shrapnel shells were not accurate enough to cut through the wire.

In 1916 Britain developed Fuze 106, a mechanism designed to detonate a shell when it made contact with any object, including soft ground and barbed wire. It went into general service in 1917.

The creeping barrage

Developed to improve infantry attacks, the **creeping barrage** involved artillery shelling enemy positions before the infantry began their attack. As the infantry moved forwards, the artillery increased the distance of their guns every few minutes to attack any retreating enemy soldiers.

The success of a creeping barrage was dependent on the infantry achieving their objectives. Frequent and accurate reports from the front line to the artillery were necessary, but communications by phone were often lost.

The effects of new technology

Some innovations in warfare, especially the machine gun and Fuze 106, were very effective on the battlefield. By contrast the tank, still at an early stage of development, failed to provide Britain with a weapon to break the deadlock on the Western Front. It was only in late 1918 that these new instruments of warfare all acted together to make a convincing break in the German lines.

Simple essay style

Below is a sample exam-style question. Use your own knowledge and the information on the opposite page to produce a plan for this question. Choose four general points and provide three pieces of specific information to support each general point. Once you have planned your essay, write the introduction and conclusion for the essay. The introduction should list the points to be discussed in the essay. The conclusion should summarise the key points and justify which point was the most important.

> How accurate would it be to true to say that the British Army quickly adjusted to the problems of trench warfare in the years 1914 to 1916?

 You're the examiner

Below are a sample exam-style question and a paragraph written in answer to the question. Read the paragraph and the mark scheme provided on pages 94–5. Decide which level you would award the paragraph. Write the level below along with a justification for your choice.

> To what extent was British artillery responsible for the BEF's success in the First World War?

Planes and tanks played their part, but British artillery superiority gave the BEF a crucial advantage in the Hundred Days Offensive. By 1918 enormous strides had been made in the use of the creeping barrage. Further advances in mapping, aerial photography, surveying and communication helped to produce accurate fire. Specialised shells were also important. The 106 fuse, for example, caused shells to explode on the slightest contact and to expend their blast horizontally, thereby cutting barbed wire. But in many ways it was the sheer quantity of guns and shells that paved the way for the BEF's success. By August 1918 the BEF fired ten or twenty shells for every one they received back from the enemy.

Level:

Reason for choosing this level and this mark

_____

_____

Public perceptions of, and changing attitudes to, the war on the Western Front

The media and propaganda

The government did its best to shape opinion and maintain the British public's commitment to the war.

Newspaper censorship

In 1914, the government was concerned that newspapers might divulge information to the enemy. Therefore:

- Newspapers publishing unauthorised news ran the risk of prosecution.
- No war correspondents followed the army to France in 1914. In 1915, six correspondents were invited to GHQ 'for a limited period'. They remained in this privileged position until 1918. Journalists were forbidden from going to the front line of action and could not report on military campaigns.
- A press bureau was established. It distributed statements from GHQ and government departments, and also advised on the publication of other news.
- In 1915, many national and local newspapers began to publish full lists of war casualties. This practice was discontinued two years later, amid fears that such lists might demoralise the population and influence public attitudes towards the war.
- Photographs taken on the Western Front were strictly controlled.

In practice, the press, which generally took a patriotic line, largely censored itself. The **D-Notice system**, introduced to warn newspapers off 'sensitive' topics, was rarely employed.

Government propaganda

- The Parliamentary Recruiting Committee (PRC) produced 50 million posters and other publications, as well as hosting countless rallies. This must have had some effect but, given the first dramatic surge in recruiting took place before the PRC was established, it is likely the PRC was preaching to the converted.
- In 1914, the government established a bureau at Wellington House, in its first direct propaganda initiative. Wellington House directed its propaganda almost entirely at opinion in neutral countries.
- In 1917, a Department of Information was set up (becoming a full ministry in 1918). The department/ministry was more concerned with international than home opinion.
- Worried by what it saw as flagging commitment at home, the government established a National War Aims Committee in 1917. The Committee issued literature, printed posters and organised speakers to address public meetings.

Non-government propaganda

Much propaganda was generated by private individuals, firms and agencies:

- Journalists, academics, writers and film-makers produced huge amounts of anti-German material.
- A variety of groups campaigned for British victory.

German actions

Arguably, German actions constituted the most effective propaganda. The invasion of Belgium, the savage treatment of some of its people and the naval bombardment of east coast towns created intense anger in 1914. Thereafter, whenever it seemed enthusiasm for the war was flagging, Germany did something sufficiently barbarous to confirm Britons in the belief that they were fighting a just war.

Opposition to the war

Opponents of the war were small in number and far from united.

Socialist opposition

In 1914, the British Socialist Party was the only political party to call for an immediate end to hostilities. The party had few members and performed poorly in by-elections.

Conscientious objectors

Britain and the USA were the only combatant nations to recognise conscientious objectors. Those objecting to military service (only 0.33 per cent of the men in the armed services) stated their case before tribunals. Over 80 per cent were given some form of exemption. 90 per cent of those whose claims for exemption were rejected, accepted an alternative form of national service. The 1,300 'absolutists' who refused all service were drafted into military units and imprisoned by court martial when they refused to obey orders.

The threat of class war

'Troublemakers' within the industrial working class concerned the government more than pacifists. Although left-wing activism increased (especially after the Russian Revolutions of 1917), industrial unrest did not translate into serious political action.

Support or challenge?

Below is a sample exam-style question which asks how far you agree with a specific statement. Below this is a series of general statements which are relevant to the question. Using your own knowledge and the information on the opposite page, decide whether these statements support or challenge the statement in the question and tick the appropriate box.

'Gullible Britons were manipulated into supporting the First World War by government propaganda.' How far do you agree with this view?

	Support	Challenge
The government introduced the D-Notice system.		
The government created a Ministry of Information.		
Most newspapers took a patriotic line.		
A National War Aims Committee was established in 1917.		
British film-makers produced some 250 pro-British war films.		
Large numbers of men volunteered for the army in August and September 1914.		
German atrocities created outrage in Britain.		
A press bureau was established.		

Introducing an argument

Below are a sample exam-style question, a list of key points to be made in the essay and a simple introduction and conclusion to the essay. Read the question, the plan and the introduction and conclusion. Rewrite the introduction and conclusion in order to develop an argument.

'There was relatively little opposition to the First World War in Britain.' How far do you agree with this statement?

Key points
- Political opponents of the war
- Conscientious objectors
- Militant workers
- Government propaganda
- British patriotism
- German actions

Introduction

There were a number of organisations that opposed the war and campaigned for peace. However, pacifists — a word used for the first time — were few in number and far from united.

Conclusion

Thus most Britons supported the First World War from start to finish. British morale remained high throughout the war. Opponents of the war never won much support.

The significance of Haig's major offensives for the conduct of the war

The Somme, July–November 1916

In December 1915, **Douglas Haig** became Commander-in-Chief of Britain's forces and held this position until the end of the war. Haig was a firm believer in maintaining an offensive strategy against the German armies.

In 1916, Kitchener's New Armies poured into France. In an effort to take pressure off France, which was fighting against fierce German attacks at Verdun, Haig agreed to a combined Anglo-French operation on the River Somme.

The artillery bombardment

The Somme battle commenced in late June with a week-long bombardment of German lines. Unfortunately, British artillery did not have enough heavy guns or the right type of shells and the bombardment both failed to cut German barbed wire and left deep dug-outs largely untouched.

The first day

1 July began with an Allied artillery barrage of 600,000 shells, fired by 1,500 guns. At 7.30 a.m., 14 British and three French divisions advanced. Unfortunately, the artillery barrage was too far ahead, lifting over the front-line enemy trenches minutes before the British infantry could reach them. The Germans returned to the parapets and manned their machine guns before the British arrived. 19,000 British troops were killed as they advanced into a hail of fire – the greatest one-day loss in the British Army's history.

The Somme continues

Attacks on the Somme continued and, as the Germans counterattacked, their own casualties also increased. The Somme offensive was finally called off on 19 November. Britain incurred 420,000 casualties, France 194,000 and Germany 465,000. The Allies had advanced no further than seven miles.

Haig's responsibility for the Somme

While it is easy to blame Haig for the Somme, it is important to recognise the dilemma he faced. Given the need to assist France, he had no option but to attack, and the technology of war continued to operate against attacking forces. Machine guns, positioned in trenches and protected by barbed wire, gave defenders a massive advantage. Heavy artillery bombardment was needed if the attackers were to have any chance of a breakthrough – but such a bombardment warned the enemy of a coming attack. Nor had any army yet found a foolproof way of co-ordinating artillery and infantry. Moreover, if attackers broke through the first defence line, there was a second line – and defending generals could plug gaps more quickly than the attacking side could advance. There were also problems of battlefield command. If troops advanced in close order they were mown down. If they advanced in open order, officers lost control of them.

Complete the paragraph **a**

Below are a sample exam-style question and a paragraph written in answer to this question. The paragraph contains a point and a concluding explanatory link back to the question, but lacks examples. Complete the paragraph, adding examples in the space provided.

'The Battle of the Somme was a total disaster for the British Army.' How far do you agree with this view?

On 1 July 1916, after a huge artillery barrage, 14 British infantry divisions attacked. The result was disastrous.

_____

_____

Thus, by the end of the first day of the Somme battle Britain had suffered over 57,000 casualties, including 19,000 deaths, the greatest loss of life in one day in the British Army's history. German losses were about a tenth of this. The day had thus been a tragic and terrible failure from a British perspective.

 Mind map

Use the information on the opposite page to add detail to the mind map below. This information should help you better understand the main issues and events surrounding the Somme.

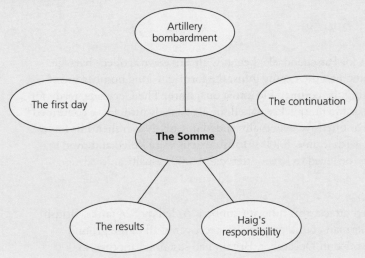

Passschendaele, July–December, 1917

The failure of Nivelle's offensive

The French General Robert Nivelle claimed that he knew how to win the war with few casualties. He so impressed Lloyd George that he was placed in supreme command over British forces for the coming offensive. That offensive was delayed by the German withdrawal to the **Hindenburg line**.

The Battle of Arras

A preliminary and diversionary offensive, the Battle of Arras (9–14 April), started well with British forces advancing three and a half miles and Canadian forces capturing Vimy Ridge. The battle, making use of the artillery's creeping barrage, was fought as series of limited attacks, leap-frogging each other, with pauses to consolidate. Arras showed that **combined arms tactics** and careful preparation could break the enemy line.

Nivelle's failure

Nivelle's offensive, delayed until mid-April, was a disaster and, following it, a large part of the French Army mutinied. Nivelle's failure vindicated Haig and Robertson's opposition to Lloyd George's project of a supreme command. Haig renewed the Arras offensive on 23 April without much success.

Haig's 'show'

By mid-1917, the BEF had replaced the French Army as the main force on the Western Front. Haig, confident that 'the German was now nearly at his last resources', was eager to launch a great offensive in Flanders. He believed British forces could break out of the Ypres **salient** and take over the entire German front. Robertson, who favoured an attritional strategy, was supportive. Lloyd George was sceptical. However:
- British success at Messines Ridge (7 June), following the detonation of a million pounds of high explosives under German trenches, was a cause for confidence.
- Fearing that a pro-peace government might come to power in France, Lloyd George accepted that Britain must do something.

Passchendaele

On 31 July, the third Battle of Ypres (or Passchendaele) began with a massive artillery barrage. While British gun batteries eliminated half the enemy guns, the fortnight-long bombardment destroyed the drainage system, turning the countryside into a quagmire. The Germans, ready for the attack which followed the bombardment, quickly halted the British advance. Haig continued to mount a series of costly attacks. His offensive eventually ended in early November. His forces had advanced no more than 10,000 yards. Some 70,000 British troops were killed and over 170,000 wounded. The Germans are believed to have suffered 200,000 casualties.

Cambrai

In November, Haig launched another attack, this time at Cambrai. Aided by 324 tanks, British troops advanced over three miles. German counterattacks later recovered all of the ground previously lost. When the fighting ended in December, Britain had sustained another 45,000 casualties.

Below is a sample exam question with the accompanying source. Having read the question and the source, complete the following activity.

> Assess the value of Source 1 for revealing the military situation in mid-1917 and the approach of Field-Marshal Douglas Haig to that situation. Explain your answer, using the source, the information given about its origin and your own knowledge about the historical content.

First, look for aspects of the source that refer to events and/or discussions that were going on around the time that the source was written. Underline the key phrases and write a brief description of the context in the margin next to the source. Draw an arrow from the key phrase to the context. Try and find at least three key phrases from the source.

Tip: look at the information above the source. You should contextualise this too. Pay particular attention to the date on which the source was written.

SOURCE 1

This is an extract from Present Situation and Future Plans, *a document written by Field-Marshal Douglas Haig on 12 June 1917. Haig hoped to convince Lloyd George and the War Council to support his plan for a great attack in Flanders later in the summer.*

At the present crisis of the war French hope must have something to feed on. The hope of American assistance is not sufficient for this purpose. It is still too far distant and the French are living a good deal on the hope of further British successes. They can and will assist in these by keeping the enemy on their front fully employed, wearing him down, and preventing him from withdrawing divisions to oppose us. But they feel unable at present to do more than this, and it is useless to expect it of them – although any considerable British successes, and signs of a breakdown in the German power of resistance, would probably have an electrifying effect.

That the British armies in France are capable of gaining considerable further success this year I am confident, as are all ranks under my command; - it is only the extent of the success that is possible that is in doubt, and that depends mainly on three factors, viz:

Firstly on whether the War Cabinet decides to concentrate our resources on the effort.

Secondly, on the degree of help given by Russia.

Thirdly, on the extent to which the German resolution and power of endurance stand the great strain they are undergoing.

The first of these factors lies within the power of the War Cabinet. The second to some extent, and the third to a very great extent, depend on their decisions.

It is my considered opinion, based not on mere optimism but on a thorough study of the situation, guided by experience which I may claim to be considerable, that if our resources are concentrated in France to the fullest possible extent the British armies are capable and can be relied on to effect great results this summer – results which will make final victory more assured and which may even bring it within reach this year.

The Hundred Days Offensive, 1918

The situation in 1918

Peace with Russia enabled Germany to transfer men to the west.

The British Army in 1918

- In 1917, casualties and injuries resulted in a 'wastage' level of 76,000 men a month on the Western Front; the army faced a manpower crisis. Resupplying this manpower, however, was low on the government's list of priorities. Haig wanted 600,000 new men: he was promised 100,000.
- British factories continued to produce great quantities of weaponry.

The Ludendorff Spring Offensive

General Ludendorff was determined to launch a German offensive strike before the Americans arrived in overwhelming numbers.

German success

Ludendorff's attack on the Somme (21 March) took the British by surprise. There was no warning bombardment beforehand. Specially trained troops broke through weak spots in the Allied line. Instead of consolidating these positions, they pressed forward rapidly and bypassed allied frontline units, which were dealt with later by supporting troops. British troops fell back over 40 miles.

Allied co-operation

On 3 April, French Marshal Foch was appointed Allied Commander-in-Chief, with the task of co-ordinating the operations of the Allied armies. However, without a staff, his appointment had a limited impact.

The failure of Ludendorff's Offensive

Fortunately for the Allies, the German offensive began to lose momentum.
- In April, the BEF repelled German attacks on Amiens and Flanders.
- The BEF was strengthened by 500,000 troops from Britain, Palestine and Italy.
- US troops, arriving in France at the rate of 250,000 a month, fought alongside five British divisions and helped staunch a German advance on Paris.

The Hundred Days Offensive

By July, the Germans had exhausted their resources. Both Haig and Foch were now keen to attack.

Amiens

On 8 August at Amiens (dubbed by Ludendorff 'the black day of the German Army'), a BEF attack gained eight miles (13 km) and inflicted 27,000 casualties, losing only 8,000 men. British troops continued to press forward.

Reasons for British success

- Britain now outgunned the Germans. At Amiens, Haig had 2,000 guns, 450 tanks and 1,900 planes.
- The various military branches – artillery, infantry, machine guns, tanks, gas and aircraft – coordinated effectively.
- British artillery, skilled in surveying and creeping barrage techniques, and using a variety of specialised shells, played a crucial role.
- Rather than aiming to capture pre-set objectives, the 1918 offensives took place across a wide front with the centre of attack repeatedly switched from one area to another, preventing German resistance solidifying.

British advance

Despite facing stiff German resistance – from 21 August to 11 November the BEF incurred 264,383 casualties, a daily loss of 3,645 men – the BEF pushed on. During this period, on 29 September, British troops crossed a seemingly impregnable part of the Hindenburg line. The attack followed a 56-hour artillery bombardment, using 1,637 guns on a 10,000-yard front. Almost a million shells were fired in a 24-hour period.

German defeat

By November, Germany's forces were retreating, its allies had surrendered and revolution forced Kaiser Wilhelm II to abdicate. A new German government accepted the Allies' **armistice** terms and the war ended on 11 November.

Military losses

Britain lost 750,000 (1.5 per cent of the pre-war population). Unlike earlier wars, most deaths were due to battle, not disease. British soldiers benefited from the use of antiseptics and from a mass inoculation programme. Improved anaesthetic and X-ray techniques, blood-transfusion developments and the work of the Medical Service Corps contributed to a high recovery rate from wounds.

Simple essay style

Below is a sample exam-style question. Use your own knowledge and the information on the opposite page to produce a plan for this question. Choose four general points and provide three pieces of specific information to support each general point. Once you have planned your essay, write the introduction and conclusion for the essay. The introduction should list the points to be discussed in the essay. The conclusion should summarise the key points and justify which point was the most important.

> How accurate would it be to say that the British Army was responsible for German defeat in November 1918?

You're the examiner

Below are a sample exam-style question and a paragraph written in answer to the question. Read the paragraph and the mark scheme provided on pages 94–5. Decide which level you would award the paragraph. Write the level below along with a justification for your choice.

> To what extent was British artillery responsible for the BEF's success in the Hundred Days Offensive in 1918?

> Planes and tanks played their part, but British artillery superiority gave the BEF a crucial advantage in the Hundred Days Offensive. By 1918 enormous strides had been made in the use of the creeping barrage. Further advances in mapping, aerial photography, surveying and communication helped to produce accurate fire. Specialised shells were also important. The 106 fuse, for example, caused shells to explode on the slightest contact and to expend their blast horizontally, thereby cutting barbed wire. But in many ways it was the sheer quantity of guns and shells that paved the way for the BEF's success. By August 1918 the BEF fired ten or twenty shells for every one they received back from the enemy.

Level:

Reason for choosing this level and this mark

_____

_____

Exam focus

Below are an exam-style question and model answer. Read it and the comments around it.

To what extent did Douglas Haig prove himself an effective commander during the years 1914 to 1918?

Haig remains one of the most controversial figures in British military history. Many at the time, and since, have criticised his leadership. Today Haig is often portrayed as an inept commander who exhibited callous disregard for his men's lives. However, Haig has his defenders. Many American and British military historians have portrayed him as one of Britain's greatest soldiers. So how effective a commander was Haig?

Haig had advanced in the army by virtue of hard work and professionalism. He fought in the Sudan in 1898 and in the Second Boer War. He served on the Western Front in 1914–15. He did not cover himself in glory at the Battle of Loos (September 1915), losing 50,000 casualties in a fruitless attack on German trenches. Despite this failure, he replaced Sir John French as commander-in-chief of the BEF in December 1915. He was a more stable character than French and unruffled by defeat. He thought that his role was to set strategy and then let his corps commanders get on with the job with minimal interference.

It is easy to blame Haig for the Somme. But his critics were unwilling to recognise the dilemma he faced. Doing nothing would have sown doubts in French minds about the seriousness of Britain's commitment. Haig had to attack. And the technology of war continued to operate against attacking forces. Machine guns, positioned in trenches protected by barbed wire, gave defenders a massive advantage. Heavy artillery bombardment was needed if attackers were to have any chance of making a breakthrough – but such a bombardment warned the enemy of a coming attack. Nor had any army yet found a way of coordinating artillery and infantry. There were also problems of battlefield command and communication. Generals, Haig included, were unable to control the operations they set in progress. The Somme offensive was reliant on the effective use of the creeping barrage – a military tactic not yet perfected. After more than four months of fighting – and 420,000 British casualties – the Allies had advanced no further than seven miles.

In 1917, Haig thought the Germans were near the end of their resources and believed that an offensive in Flanders could win the war. Most of Britain's war leaders supported Haig's 'show' and, on 31 July, the third Battle of Ypres – known as Passchendaele – was launched. A massive, two-week-long, opening barrage destroyed the Flanders drainage system and turned the countryside into a quagmire. A German defence-in-depth scheme halted the British advance in its tracks. By the end of the offensive in November British forces had advanced no more than 10,000 yards. Some 70,000 British troops were killed and over 170,000 wounded.

The introduction displays a good understanding of the question, uses quotes to good effect and interestingly sits on the fence with regard to the way the essay is likely to go. Will it support Haig or will it criticise him?

A succinct paragraph which deals with Haig's military career before he became commander-in-chief of the BEF. It could perhaps do with a final sentence which links back to the question.

A reasoned and reasonable defence of the situation facing Haig in 1916. The candidate continues to sit on the defence with regard to Haig's effectiveness. No bad thing – but it is not always an easy or comfortable position to adopt.

This paragraph continues to demonstrate a good understanding of the situation in 1917. Again, no link back to the question. But it could be that the stark last sentence is sufficient.

In late November, Haig authorised another an attack at Cambrai. A short but very accurate bombardment eliminated German guns, and the following attack took the enemy by surprise. British troops advanced over three miles. German counterattacks later recovered this ground however and, for the first time, newspapers started to voice criticisms of Haig. Despite this, War Minister Jan Smuts, after touring the Western Front, reported – of Haig – that there was no one better. In the spring of 1918, German troops drove the British back over 40 miles. On 11 April, Haig issued his 'Backs to the Wall' order, declaring British troops must fight to the end. The BEF held out, preventing the Germans capturing vital Channel ports.

> This paragraph makes some sensible points about Haig's effectiveness but is something of a filler. We still don't know the opinion of the essay on Haig. Perhaps it might have emphasised Smuts' claim that there was no one better.

In the summer of 1918, the situation changed massively in Haig's favour. German resources were exhausted while the BEF were well-supplied with both traditional arms and a variety of new weapons. Haig's Hundred Days Offensive (August–November 1918) showed considerable skills in generalship. Tactics were also changed. Rather than aiming to capture predetermined objectives, the offensives took place cross a wide front with the centre of attack repeatedly switched from one area to another, preventing German resistance solidifying. His most impressive victory was at Amiens on 8 August. When a new German government agreed to an armistice in November, Germany still controlled most of Belgium and large parts of France. Haig's military success, therefore, had been far from total. Moreover, throughout the Hundred Days Offensive he had continued to lose 3,645 men a day.

> Haig is given some credit but the fence remains straddled. The essay thus continues to be consistent.

The debate about Haig's military effectiveness looks set to continue. It is easy to blame Haig for his rigid command style and for the hundreds of thousands of men he squandered in battle. However, in Haig's defence, he pursued the only possible strategy in 1916–17, given the military and political situation. Arguably his tactics did wear down the Germans, enabling him to deliver the knockout blow in 1918. Historian Gary Sheffield has called the Hundred Days Offensive 'by far the greatest military victory in British history'. By November 1918 the British Army was the most highly mechanised in the world. It was also the most successful in the last months of the war. Enormous strides had been made in the use of the creeping barrage, in survey techniques and in the use of combined arms tactics. For all of this, Haig must surely take some credit.

> The conclusion is strong. The essay has argued that there are good things to say about Haig and bad things to say, and has (very effectively) said both – no easy thing to do.

This falls between a Level 4 and a Level 5 essay. It is certainly well written and demonstrates a detailed and wide-ranging knowledge of the topic and a very good understanding of the question. However, the analysis is sometimes lost in the detail and is not fully sustained. Links back to the question at the end of each paragraph would help.

Moving from a Level 4 to Level 5

The exam focus essay at the end of Section 2 (pages 30–31) provided a Level 5 essay. The essay here achieves a Level 4/5. Read both essays and the comments provided. Make a list of the additional features required to push a Level 4 essay into Level 5.

Aircraft development

REVISED

Orville and Wilbur Wright had managed to get an aeroplane airborne in 1903. By 1914, aircraft development had taken huge strides and all the major powers realised aircraft's military potential. Nevertheless, the aircraft available to both sides in 1914 were rudimentary. The British FE-2a, for example, could manage a top speed of no more than 88kph (55mph).

In 1914, Britain had 113 aircraft, France 160, and Germany 246.

Aerial reconnaissance

The main use of aircraft was for reconnaissance. Over 90 per cent of aerial sorties flown throughout the war were reconnaissance missions. The role of Allied airmen in detecting German troop movements that led to the Battle of the Marne demonstrated the aeroplane's value. When trench warfare began in 1914, aircraft were used to spot enemy artillery, while aerial photographic reconnaissance enabled accurate maps of enemy trenches to be created. Reconnaissance aircraft became increasingly sophisticated.

- Reconnaissance reports were increasingly delivered by radio rather than in person.
- Bulky hand-held cameras gave way to smaller cameras fitted within the fuselage.
- New types of planes could fly higher and faster.

Balloons

Tethered balloons had a key battlefield role. Equipped with telephones and binoculars, observers could see very long distances into enemy-held territory from their baskets, generating valuable information. As such they tended to be a priority target for attacking aircraft and were, therefore, heavily defended.

Fighters

As the value of air reconnaissance became apparent, both sides began to develop fighter aircraft whose main role was to shoot down enemy aircraft and protect friendly reconnaissance aircraft. The first fighters were two-seater planes, fitted with a single machine-gun operated by the observer from the rear of the cockpit. The chief problem was that the machine-gun was easiest to aim when firing forward. However, most aircraft had a wooden propeller at the front of the fuselage and there was no means of firing through its arc without shooting the wood to pieces.

In 1915, the French fitted steel plates to their propellers which deflected bullets away without causing damage. However, in mid-1915 the Germans produced a device that prevented a machine-gun from firing when a propeller blade passed immediately in front of its barrel. This gave the Germans a crucial advantage in the second half of 1915, and their Fokker planes shot down more than 1,000 Allied aircraft.

Allied air superiority, 1916

As a result of the 1915 'Fokker Scourge', British leaders recognised the need for a larger and better equipped Royal Flying Corps (RFC). The creation of new British fighter squadrons was one thing, quite another was the production of good quality aircraft and the training of new pilots. However, by the Battle of the Somme (July 1916), Britain had developed new types of aircraft (such as the Sopwith 1 ½ Strutter) that were as good, if not better than German planes. The Allies had aerial superiority for most of late 1916.

Simple essay style

Below is a sample exam-style question. Use your own knowledge and the information on the opposite page to produce a plan for this question. Choose four general points and provide three pieces of specific information to support each general point. Once you have planned your essay, write the information and conclusion for the essay. The conclusion should summarise the key points and justify which point was the most important.

How significant was the role of aircraft in the years 1914–16?

 You're the examiner

Below are a sample exam-style question and a paragraph written in answer to the question. Read the paragraph and the mark scheme provided on pages 94–5. Describe which level you would award the paragraph. Write the level below, along with a justification for your choice.

'Aircraft played an insignificant role in the years 1914–16.' How far do you agree with this view?

Between 1914 and 1916, the main use of aircraft was for reconnaissance. Over 90 per cent of aerial sorties were reconnaissance missions. The role of Allied airmen in detecting German troop movements that led to the Battle of the Marne in 1914 demonstrated the aeroplane's value. When trench warfare began, aircraft were used to spot enemy artillery, while aerial photographic reconnaissance enabled accurate maps of enemy trenches to be created. Reconnaissance aircraft became increasingly sophisticated. New types of planes could fly higher and faster while reconnaissance reports were increasingly delivered by radio rather than in person. While aircraft undoubtedly played an important reconnaissance role, it was a role that was hardly likely to determine the outcome of the First World War. In 1916 most experts knew that the War's outcome would be decided by the soldiers on the ground.

Level:

Reason for choosing this level and this mark

_____

_____

The importance of air power in Britain's victory by 1918

The aerial war, 1917–18

Under the pressure of war, aircraft development was accelerated and new methods of waging aerial war were introduced.

Ground-attack

Close co-operation between ground and air units became an important part of offensive operations. Given that few planes were built specifically as ground-attack aircraft, both sides generally used bombers and fighters for close-support missions. Such missions had a limited impact:

- Aerial bombing tended to be inaccurate.
- Pilots and their unprotected aircraft were highly vulnerable to machine-gun and rifle fire as they swooped down to strafe enemy positions.

The importance of reconnaissance

Reconnaissance remained aircraft's most vital work. Indirect artillery fire – shooting at targets not visible from gun batteries – became possible because aeroplanes flew over enemy positions and identified targets. Gunners, aided by accurate maps produced by aerial photographs, were also guided by airmen who used radio to direct artillery fire. The main task of fighter aircraft was still to shoot down reconnaissance planes.

Technological development

The fighter planes of 1917–18 were far superior to their predecessors. Fitted with more powerful engines, they had a better rate of climb, greater speed and were more manoeuvrable. The air war was thus essentially a technological struggle. Air superiority switched back and forth as new planes outclassed older opponents. This was demonstrated in the Battle of Arras (see page 54). While the British enjoyed a three to one advantage in aircraft, their BE-2s and RE-8s were no match for the German Albatros D-types. During April 1917, the RFC lost 151 aircraft and 316 crew compared to German losses of 66 planes and 119 crew. However, the D-types were soon outclassed by British planes.

- Between May and September 1917, five Sopwith Triplanes downed 87 German aircraft without loss.
- By late 1917, Britain was producing the Sopwith F-1 Camel. The first British aircraft to be built with two synchronised machine-guns, it became Britain's leading fighter for the remainder of the war, shooting down some 1,300 enemy aircraft.

Aces

Fighter pilots developed the tactics of air combat. Victory usually went to pilots who exploited the sun and clouds to sneak up behind opponents and open fire at close range. Pilots who achieved more than five 'kills' were recognized as 'aces'. As well as being expert pilots and skilled marksmen, the great 'aces' invariably had better aircraft than their opponents. The aces' activities captured the public's imagination and became the focus of propaganda campaigns to boost morale. While aerial combat was seen as gallant and chivalrous, in reality it was bloody and highly dangerous.

The Western Front

Aircraft made an important contribution to Haig's success in 1918. By 1918, the Allies were producing over 11,000 planes a month while the Germans manufactured below 2,000. Control of the skies allowed the Allies to reconnoitre battlefields with impunity. Aircraft also provided tactical support for infantry and launched raids on enemy supply lines, communication centres and reserves.

Mind map

Use the information on the opposite page to add detail to the mind map. This should assist your understanding of the significance of aircraft's role in 1917–18.

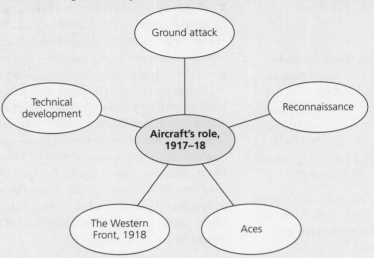

 Complete the paragraph a

Below are a sample exam-style question and a paragraph written in answer to the question. The paragraph contains a point and specific examples, but lacks a concluding explanatory link back to the question. Complete the paragraph, adding the link in the space provided.

'By 1918 aircraft played a major role in Allied victory.' How far do you agree with this view?

Aircraft made an important contribution to Douglas Haig's success in the Hundred Days Offensive between August and November 1918. By 1918 the Allies were producing over 11,000 planes a month while the Germans manufactured less than 2000. Control of the skies allowed the Allies to reconnoitre battlefields with impunity. Aircraft provided British artillery with valuable information about the placement of German guns and the strength of German defences. They could also provide tactical support for infantry and launch raids on enemy supply lines, communication centres and reserves.

_____

_____

The bombing of civilian targets

German bombing of Britain

The First World War saw the bombing of British cities.

Zeppelin bombing

At the start of the twentieth century, Germany had embraced the airship for both military and civilian use. An airship programme was launched and presided over by Count Ferdinand von Zeppelin. On 19–20 January 1915, two Zeppelins bombed Great Yarmouth and King's Lynn, killing five people. London was bombed by Zeppelins in May 1915. There were a further 19 missions in 1915, 22 in 1916, seven in 1917 and four in 1918.

In all, 556 British civilians were killed and 1,350 injured by the 5,750 bombs dropped from Zeppelins. Although relatively trivial, the raids caused some interruption.
● Lighting restrictions were imposed
● Factories stopped work when raiders were sighted.

However, as British defences improved, Zeppelins became vulnerable to anti-aircraft guns and fighter aircraft, as well as adverse weather.

Aeroplane bombing

Although there had been German aircraft raids on England since 1914, true strategic bombing did not begin until 1917. German leaders hoped to crush Britain's will to fight by disrupting war industry, communications and supply. The first raid on London occurred during daylight on 27 May 1917. Seven more raids followed. On 13 June, 162 people were killed in London in a raid by 14 Gothas.

While the raids caused alarm, Germany lacked sufficient planes to cause serious disruption to Britain's war effort. As Britain's anti-aircraft defences improved, German bombers suffered heavy losses. In August, the Gothas turned to night operations, which were safer but less accurate. There were a further 19 raids, the final one coming on 19–20 May 1918. British civilian casualties totalled around 850 dead and 2,000 injured.

The RAF

While many Britons demanded bombing attacks on German towns in reprisal for attacks on Britain, aerial experts opposed the idea, convinced that planes were best used in cooperation with the army. General **Jan Smuts,** given the task of judging air power, claimed, in October 1917, that, given enough planes, Germany could be bombed into submission. Lloyd George and Churchill, whose minds were always open to innovation, liked the idea. An independent air ministry was set up under Lord Rothermere, the younger brother of Viscount Northcliffe, the press magnate. In April 1918, the Royal Air Force (RAF) was formed. It was the world's first air service that was independent of either an army or navy. Major-General Hugh Trenchard, head of the RFC, was made chief of staff to the RAF.

British bombing of Germany

By the summer of 1918, British bombers, using French airfields, regularly struck at targets located in the industrial heartland of western Germany. In total, Britain dropped 665 tons of bombs on Germany, losing 450 planes in the process. By late 1918, Trenchard was planning to launch raids deep into Germany, hoping to bomb the country into submission. However, the Allies did not have enough planes to do major damage to Germany's infrastructure or to German morale.

The impact of bombing on public opinion

The bombing of cities, although disruptive, had little impact on the war's outcome. Indeed, in some ways it may have been counter-productive.
● It cost far more to build planes (or Zeppelins) and send them on bombing missions than the damage they inflicted.
● It provided useful propaganda material for the British press.
● German bombing helped strengthen the people's belief that they were engaged in a righteous cause against a barbarous enemy.

Spectrum of significance

Below are a sample exam-style question and a list of general points which could be used to answer the question. Use your own knowledge and the information on the opposite page to reach a judgement about the importance of these general points to the question posed. Write numbers on the spectrum to indicate their relative importance. Having done this, write a brief justification of your placement, explaining why some of these factors are more important than others. The resulting diagram could form the basis of an essay plan.

To what extent was German bombing of British civilians counter-productive?

←——————————————————————————————→

Bombing successful   Bombing a failure

1   The Zeppelin bombing

2   German aeroplane bombing

3   German losses

4   The effect on the British public

5   The establishment of the RAF

6   The cost of bombing

7   British bombing of Germany

Develop the detail   a

Below are a sample exam-style question and the paragraph written in answer to the question. The paragraph contains a limited amount of detail. Annotate the paragraph to add additional detail to the answer.

'Bombing of civilians by both sides had little effect.' How far do you agree with this view of aerial bombing in the First World War?

German aircraft raids on England did not commence on a major scale until 1917. London was first bombed on 27 May 1917. German High Command's aim to crush Britain's will and ability to fight came to nothing. Indeed the air attacks may have strengthened the resolve of most Britons to continue the war.

Exam focus

Below are a sample source, question and answer to the question. Read the source. Then read the answer and the comments around it.

Assess the value of Source 1 for revealing information about the establishment of the Royal Air Force and for revealing the British government's attitudes to air power in the summer of 1917. Explain your answer using the sources, the information given about its origin and your own knowledge about the historical context.

SOURCE 1

This source is an extract from the Second Report of the Prime Minister's Committee on Air Organisation and Home Defence against Air Raids. *The Committee meeting at which the report was discussed was held on 17 August 1917. General Jan Smuts, a South African whom Lloyd George had appointed to his war cabinet, was the driving force behind the Report. Lloyd George had given him the task of assessing the future role of Britain's air force, following the panic created by major German air raids on Britain in the summer of 1917.*

At the 181st Meeting, held on 11th July 1917, the War Cabinet decided –

'That the Prime Minister and General Smuts in consultation with representatives of the Admiralty, General Staff and Field Marshal Commanding-in-Chief, Home Forces, with such other experts as they may desire, should examine –

1) The defence arrangements for Home Defence against air raids.

2) The air organisation generally and the direction of aerial operations.

5) The time is, however, rapidly approaching when that subordination of the Air Board and the Air Service could no longer be justified. Essentially the position of an Air service is quite different from that of an artillery arm, to pursue our comparison; artillery could never be used in war except as a weapon in military or naval or air operations. It is a weapon, an instrument ancillary to a service, but could not be an independent service itself. Air service on the contrary can be used as an independent means of war operations. Nobody that witnessed the attack on London on 11th July could have any doubt on that point. Unlike artillery, an air fleet can conduct extensive operations far from, and independently of, both Army and Navy. As far as can at present be foreseen there is absolutely no limit to the scale of its future independent war use. And the day may not be far off when aerial operations with their devastation of enemy lands and destruction of industrial and populous centres on a vast scale may become the principal operations of war, to which the older forces of military and naval operations may become secondary and subordinate. The subjection of the Air Board and service could only be justified on the score of their infancy. But this is a disability which time can remove, and in this respect the march of events has been very rapid during the war. In our opinion there is no reason why the Air Board should any longer continue in its present form as practically no more than a conference room between the older services, and there is every reason why it should be raised to the status of an independent Ministry in control of its own war service.

6) The urgency for the change will appear from the following facts, Hitherto aircraft production has been insufficient to supply the demands of both Army and Navy, and the chief concerns of the Air Board has been to satisfy the necessary requirements of those services. But that phase is rapidly passing. The programme of aircraft production which the War Cabinet has sanctioned for the following twelve months is far in excess of Navy and Army requirements. Next spring and summer the position will be that the Army and Navy will have all the Air service required in connection with their operations; and over and above that there will be a great surplus available for independent operations. Who is to look after and direct the activities of this available surplus? Neither the Army nor the Navy is specially competent to do so; and for that reason the creation of an Air Staff for planning and directing independent air operations will soon be pressing.

This source provides invaluable information about the establishment of the Royal Air Force. From 1914 to 1917 the army and navy had controlled Britain's fledgling air power. The main use of aircraft had been reconnaissance: from 1914 aircraft were used to spot enemy artillery, while aerial photographic reconnaissance enabled accurate maps of enemy trenches to be created. Once the value of air reconnaissance became apparent, both sides began to develop fighter aircraft whose main role was to shoot down enemy aircraft and protect friendly reconnaissance aircraft. By 1917 aircraft began to play an increasingly important role on the battlefield.

A safe, sensible and well-written introduction which provides some context to the source.

Following German Gotha raids on Britain in the summer of 1917, there were demands for reprisals. General Jan Smuts, as Source 1 makes clear, was instructed to examine Britain's defence arrangements against German air attacks on British towns. He was also asked to examine air organisation generally and the future direction of aerial operations. Smuts argued that air fleets could conduct extensive operations far from, and independently of, both the army and the navy. He also believed that, by 1918, Britain would have more planes than the army and navy actually required, and that neither the military branch were capable of directing the activities of these surplus planes. His radical proposal was that Britain's Air Service should become an independent force.

This paragraph is a good mix of contextual knowledge and sound paraphrasing of the source.

Lloyd George, the Prime Minister, and Winston Churchill, Minister of Munitions, approved Smuts' proposals following his influential report. In April 1918, the Royal Air Force (RAF) was formed and, as such, Source 1 is vital to our understanding behind its creation. The source also provides evidence for some of Smuts' thinking though, it should be said, he was careful in his use of words. One motive for the creation of an independent air force was to end the inter-service rivalries that at times had adversely affected aircraft production. Another was to ensure that the navy's underutilised planes and pilots were fully employed. Neither of these things are specifically stated by Smuts however, presumably to avoid antagonising either the army or Admiralty.

This paragraph is well informed and makes some excellent inferences with regard to what Smuts does not say in this part of his report.

Source I also provides us with excellent evidence about the British government's attitude to air power in the summer of 1917. As well as providing invaluable intelligence, aircraft were also able to provide tactical support for infantry and launch raids on enemy supply lines, communication centres and reserves. The huge efforts being put into the construction of aircraft – with aircraft production targeted to be above the production of any other weapon – demonstrates the government's view that aerial power was hugely important. As much as anything, the air war was a technological struggle and, by the summer of 1917, Britain was winning the technological war. Produced in late 1917, the Sopwith F-1 Camel was agile and with a good rate of climb, and the first British aircraft built with two synchronised machine-guns. It became Britain's leading fighter for the remainder of the war, shooting down some 1,300 enemy aircraft. By 1918, Britain was producing far more aircraft than Germany. The planes made an important contribution to Haig's success in the Hundred Days Offensive in 1918.

One of the main reasons for the creation of Smuts' committee was to investigate Britain's ability to defend itself from German strategic bombing. The first Gotha raid on London occurred during daylight on 27 May 1917. Seven more raids followed and caused serious alarm. However, by August 1917, it was clear that Germany lacked sufficient planes to cause serious disruption to Britain's war effort. Moreover, as British anti-aircraft defences improved, German bombers suffered heavy losses. In August, the Gothas turned to night operations which were safer but far less accurate. The fact that German air raids were less of a concern perhaps explains why there is no reference to them in the extract. However, it is likely that Smuts said something about the situation earlier in his report, given that this was one of the purposes of his committee.

Source I indicates that Smuts was convinced that aerial power was the force of the future. He foresaw a time when air power 'may become the principal operation of war, to which the older forces of military and naval operations may become secondary and subordinate.' Soon, he predicted, aircraft would be able to destroy 'industrial and populous centres on a vast scale'. The destruction of an enemy without fighting on land had instant appeal to Lloyd George and Churchill, both of whom abhorred the carnage of the Western Front. By the summer of 1918, British bombers, using French airfields, regularly struck at targets located in the industrial heartland of western Germany. In total, Britain dropped 665 tons of bombs on Germany, losing 450 planes in the process – a much greater scale of bombing than Germany had inflicted on Britain. Further plans to launch raids deep into Germany were, following Germany's acceptance of armistice terms in November 1918, never realised. Indeed, in reality Britain and its allies did not have enough planes to do major damage to Germany's infrastructure or to German morale.

In conclusion, Source I is of huge value to historians. The RAF came into existence largely because of the influence of the Smuts Report. The source also reveals Smuts' – and Lloyd George's – hopes for air power in the non-too-distant future. The belief that the First World War could be won by air power alone in 1919–20 was not realistic, but the fact that they thought it might be is interesting. Lloyd George and his government deserve credit for supporting the enormous aircraft-building programme in 1917, which did much to help Allied forces win the land war in November 1918.

A paragraph which examines the government's attitude to aircraft. Reference to the increase in aircraft production is well made and is supported by impressive contextual knowledge.

A short but important paragraph which comments on the lack of information in the source with regard to Britain's air defences and makes inferences about the matter. The inferences may be wrong with regard to the report as a whole, as is recognised, but they are certainly apt with regard to the extract.

Some excellent points are made about the notion that the war could be won by air power alone.

A neat conclusion which ties things up nicely.

This essay is an analytical response, integrating own knowledge with understanding of the source. It displays excellent knowledge of the source's context. It also has important – and interesting – things to say about the source's value in the two areas of the question. The conclusion is short but very effective. The candidate's answer is splendidly structured and is certainly well written. In consequence, it should be awarded a Level 5 mark.

What makes a good answer?

You have now considered two high-level source-based essays. Use these essays to make a bullet-pointed list of the characteristics of a top-level essay. Use this list when planning and writing your own practice essays.

6 Changes in organising the military

The military and reasons for change, 1790–1918

The Duke of York's reforms

The poor performance of the army in 1793–4 indicated the need for reform. Reforms by Frederick, Duke of York, Commander-in-Chief from 1795–1815, helped transform the service. These included:

- ending the worst excesses of the purchase system
- establishing a Military College to improve the professionalisation of the future officer class
- creating light infantry regiments.

The McNeil-Tulloch Report, 1855

During the Crimean War, army affairs commanded unprecedented public and parliamentary interest. In 1855, Sir John McNeill and Colonel Alexander Tulloch went to the Crimea to review the organisation and delivery of supplies to Balaclava. Their report was highly critical of the army's high command and of the officers in charge of the Commissariat. The Commissariat was reformed and made more professional in 1858.

Military reform, 1856–68

A major programme of barrack construction was launched after 1856, but little else was done to enhance the appeal of service life:

- Soldiers remained poorly paid.
- Military discipline remained harsh: flogging was not abolished until 1881.

Cardwell's army reforms, 1868–74

The Crimean War and the Indian Mutiny of 1857 both highlighted the inefficiency of the army and its structure, especially when compared with the powerful military forces being established in Germany.

Edward Cardwell, Secretary of State for War from 1868–74, undertook comprehensive reform of the army's organisation:

- Short-term enlistments were introduced. Infantry had an initial engagement of six years and then joined the reserve.
- The purchase system was abolished.
- Two regular battalions, two militia battalions and a quota of volunteers were based in each of 66 separate districts across the country. One of the two regular battalions was to serve abroad. The other was to be based at home.

Cardwell's economically driven reforms promised more than they delivered:

- The army lost more men than it gained by the introduction of short-service enlistments.
- The abolition of the purchase system did little to alter the social composition of the officer corps.
- The constant need for men to serve overseas put great strain on home battalions.

Haldane's reforms, 1905–12

The Boer War prompted demands for reform. This led to government investigations into military planning, recruitment and army organisation. By 1905, Germany was increasingly seen as a potential enemy. In light of this, a series of significant reforms were undertaken:

- The operational budget of the army – £28 million per year – dictated the size of the force. Haldane envisaged a two-line army:
  - an Expeditionary force of 150,000 men
  - a Territorial force, created from volunteers, militia and the **yeomanry**, to support and expand the Expeditionary force. Launched in 1907, by 1913 it had over 200,000 men.
- Existing military corps in schools and universities were reorganised into the Officer Training Corps.

The value of Haldane's reforms was shown in 1914, with the efficient mobilisation and performance of the British Expeditionary Force in the early months of the war.

The army in 1914

Army officers implemented the military reform:

- General Douglas Haig sought to improve preparedness by holding regular large-scale manoeuvres.
- General Henry Wilson formulated mobilisation plans, especially the preparation of railway timetables and shipping arrangements.

By 1914, the army had improved professionally. However:

- Army commanders underestimated the potential of the machine-gun and believed that cavalry charges would win battles.
- In mid-1914, Germany had 84 divisions, France 66 and Britain just six divisions ready for a European war.

Complete the paragraph a

Below are a question and a paragraph written as part of the answer to this question. The paragraph contains a point and a concluding explanatory link back to the question, but lacks examples. Complete the paragraph, adding examples in the space provided.

> To what extent was the British Army's organisation overhauled in the years 1793–1914?

Defeat in the American War of Independence had tarnished the British Army's image and morale. Its poor performance in 1793–4 indicated there was need for serious reform.

_____

_____

Thus by 1815 the British Army had been considerably improved. So much so, that it was the only military force in Europe not to suffer a major defeat at the hands of Napoleon.

Simple essay style

Below is a question. Use your own knowledge and the information on the opposite page to produce a plan for this question. Choose four general points and provide three pieces of specific information to support each general point. Once you have planned your essay, write the introduction and conclusion for the essay. The introduction should list the points to be discussed in the essay. The conclusion should summarise the key points and justify which point was the most important.

> 'Cardwell's reforms were the most important changes made to the British Army in the years between 1793 and 1914.' How far do you agree with this view?

The navy and changes in organisation, 1790–1914

REVISED

The navy, 1790–1854

The navy proved itself superior to all its competitors during the wars against France.

Reduction in size

After 1815, the navy was drastically reduced in size. Warships in commission fell from 713 in 1814, to 121 in 1818. By 1817, 90 per cent of commissioned officers were on half pay.

The navy's power

Despite reductions, the navy continued to rule the waves. The main fleet was stationed in European waters. Some 130 frigates and gunboats defended trade routes and the Empire.

Steam power

The navy kept up with new developments, especially the coming of steam. Paddle steamers proved their worth in the First Opium War with China (1839–42), but their twin paddles occupied too much room to mount an effective broadside. Accordingly, the navy relied mainly on sail in the 1830s and 1840s.

The screw propeller was developed in the late 1830s. Placed on the **stern**, the screw did not interfere with the broadside. *HMS Ajax*, in 1845, was the first battleship fitted with a screw propeller. *HMS Duke of Wellington*, launched in 1853, carried 131 guns and had a speed of 10 knots, making it the world's most powerful battleship.

Sir James Graham's reforms, 1832

Sir James Graham, First Lord of the Admiralty from 1830–34, introduced a number of naval reforms:

- The amalgamation of the Admiralty and the navy Board improved the navy's administration and ensured less nepotism, bribery and corruption.
- All crews were required to be skilled in gunnery. *HMS Excellent* was commissioned specially to help crews develop such skills.
- The system of automatic promotions was ended. Officers had to have two years' experience at sea before their promotion to commander.
- The civilian-run Naval Office and Victualling Board was abolished. All aspects of supply were placed under naval control.

Naval developments, 1854–1914

The navy performed well in the Crimean War and continued to dominate the world's oceans thereafter.

The need to modernise

During the late nineteenth century, virtually all the navy's vessels changed from sail and wood to steam and steel. Technological changes forced Britain to keep modernising its navy – a costly business. Warships could now be obsolete on completion.

The increasing threat

In the 1880s, France, Russia, the USA and Germany increased their navies. In 1889, Britain adopted a policy whereby its navy was to be kept up to the combined strength of the next two greatest naval powers. In 1898, Germany passed a Navy Law that would double the size of its fleet. This posed a threat to Britain's trade and security.

Admiral Fisher's reforms

Admiral Fisher was First Sea Lord from 1904–9.

The Selbourne Scheme

As Second Naval Lord (1902–3), Fisher pushed through the Selbourne Scheme. All naval officers were to be trained in common. Later they could specialise in engineering, navigation or gunnery. As they reached high rank, all would be eligible to command ships and for promotion to Admiral. Fisher hoped by this to produce a more meritocratic and less class-bound navy.

Submarines

Money-saving was a major consideration in Fisher's advocacy of submarines (first built by Britain in 1902). Twenty-five times cheaper to build than battleships, submarines had the potential to increase Britain's security by deterring invaders.

Battlecruisers and battleships

Invincible class battlecruisers were vessels that would combine a battleship's firepower with a cruiser's speed. More significant was the development of Dreadnought class battleships. These very powerful, all-big-gun ships, made all other ships virtually obsolete. The building of Dreadnoughts sparked a naval race between Britain and Germany.

Mind map

Use the information on the opposite page to add detail to the mind map below, so that you gain a greater understanding of naval developments between 1793 and 1914.

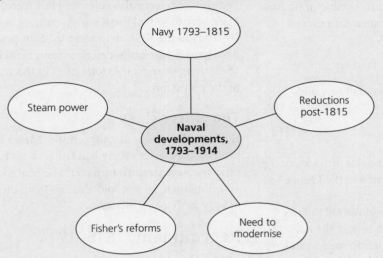

Navy 1793–1815

Steam power

Reductions post-1815

Naval developments, 1793–1914

Fisher's reforms

Need to modernise

 ## Spot the mistake

a

Below are a question and a paragraph written as part of an answer to this question. Why does the paragraph not get into Level 4? Once you have identified the mistake, rewrite the paragraph so that it displays the qualities of Level 4. The mark scheme on pages 94–5 will help you.

To what extent did the Royal Navy respond to foreign threat in the years 1793–1914?

In the early 1900s, Britain embarked on a massive programme of naval reform. This was carried through by Admiral Fisher. His reforms included overhauling the Fleet Reserve, the introduction of submarines and the building of battlecruisers and Dreadnoughts.

Recruitment of the fighting forces, 1790–1914

Recruitment, 1793–1815

Conscription was regarded as an unacceptable imposition on the liberties of Britons. Recruitment thus caused problems for the fighting forces.

The navy

After 1793, the navy's strength was usually around 120,000 men.

Naval crews

Given that voluntary recruitment did not provide enough men, the navy relied on impressment and the Quota System.

- The Impressment Service was empowered to force seafarers aged between 15 and 55 to join the navy. Press gangs were sent out to round up men in and around ports, while captains could press merchant seamen into service. By 1805, half the navy's crews were made up of pressed men.
- Each county was required to supply a certain number of volunteers, based on its population and number of seaports. To meet their quotas, counties often gave criminals the option of volunteering for the navy.

Naval officers

Most naval officers came from the professional middle classes. Many were sons or relations of naval officers. Embarking on their careers at an early age, they learned the ropes (literally) as midshipmen.

Army recruitment

No press gangs operated on the army's behalf. Finding the requisite manpower was difficult.
- Pay was poor.
- Soldiers suffered a high death rate.
- Discipline was harsh.

The Militia

The militia, which made up one-fifth of Britain's land forces, was restricted to home defence. Recruits, selected by ballot, had to serve for five years unless they paid for a substitute. After 1805, many militiamen volunteered for regular service – 74,000 between 1807 and 1812. It is thus something of a myth that the army's ranks were filled by criminals and men lured into service when drunk. Many soldiers were motivated by patriotism and the prospect of adventure.

Foreign recruitment

British Kings were also rulers of **Hanover**. Many Hanoverians joined the King's German Legion (KGL). Recruits to the KGL soon included Europeans of all descriptions, especially deserters from French armies. By 1813, there were 52,000 foreigners in the army, one-fifth of the entire force.

The officer class

By 1814, there were 10,000 officers. Most came from the professional classes. Many had fathers who had been army officers. New commissions could be attained by enlisting 40 militiamen. Men could also rise from the ranks, usually for bravery in action.

Recruitment, 1815–1914

Britain's armed forces continued to rely on volunteers.

The navy

- Given the enormous de-commissioning of ships after 1815, Britain retained – and was able to recruit – enough sailors to man its ships.
- By the late nineteenth century, the navy needed men with engineering skills or muscles to shovel coal into ships' furnaces.

The army

Although the army struggled to find enough volunteers in peacetime, patriotic sentiment ensured that Britain found sufficient men to fight in the Crimean and Boer Wars.

The army's composition

There were changes in the composition of the army.
- In 1851, Irishmen had constituted 37 per cent of all non-commissioned personnel. By 1913, the Irish element was only nine per cent.
- Demographic changes meant that the army drew increasingly on recruits from urban areas.

Army officers

One consequence of the Boer War and the German threat was the spread of cadet corps, especially in public schools. In 1908, Haldane organised these bodies into the Officer Training Corps (OTC). By 1914, some 20,000 schoolboys and 5,000 undergraduates were enrolled in the OTC.

! Eliminate irrelevance   **a**

Below are a question and a paragraph written as part of an answer to this question. Read the paragraph and identify parts of the paragraph that are not directly relevant to the question. Draw a line through the information that is irrelevant and justify your deletions in the margin.

To what extent did the British Army find it difficult to recruit in the years 1793–1914?

> Britain had major problems recruiting enough men to wage war on France in the Revolutionary and Napoleonic Wars. France, which had a system of conscription, was able to muster armies of hundreds of thousands of men. Britain could not match such numbers. In 1793, its army amounted to 40,000 men. Clearly it needed to increase its forces. But conscription was regarded as an unacceptable imposition on the liberties of freeborn Britons. The Royal Navy had similar problems recruiting. But it was entitled to use impressment. The Impressment Service had the power to force seafarers aged between 15 and 55 to join the navy. Press gangs were sent to round up suitable men in and around ports. No press gangs operated on the army's behalf. Thus, all Britain's regular soldiers were volunteers. Unfortunately, army life was not particularly attractive. Soldiers were paid less than farm workers. However, the army did offer food, drink, shelter and the prospect of loot. On top of this was a bounty — a signing-on fee — of up to £40, an important motivating factor for recruits. Even so, harsh discipline, coupled with a high death rate, made it difficult to find recruits. Most came from poor families. Soldiers were considered to be on the same level as common criminals. Indeed, some were just that. The army, the Duke of Wellington said, was 'composed of the scum of the earth...fellows who have enlisted for drink — that is the plain fact'.

! Introducing an argument

Below are a sample exam-style question, a list of key points to be made in the essay and a simple introduction and conclusion for the essay. Read the question, the plan and the introduction and conclusion. Rewrite the introduction and conclusion in order to develop an argument.

To what extent were British military forces composed of 'the scum of the earth' and officered by gentlemen in the years 1793–1914?

Key points
- The composition of the army, 1793–1815
- The composition of the navy, 1793–1815
- Changes in military recruitment, 1815–54
- The Crimean War and its aftermath
- The Boer War and its aftermath
- The situation in 1914

Introduction

> While there is clear evidence to suggest that both the army and navy were led by men of wealth throughout the years from 1793 to 1914, it is a mistake to view all Britain's ordinary soldiers and sailors as 'scum of the earth'.

Conclusion

> Thus, the social class of most army officers was similar in 1914 to that in 1793. Naval officers throughout the period tended to come more from the professional classes than the landed gentry. Most ordinary soldiers and sailors came from poor families but it would be wrong to label them as the 'scum of the earth' at any stage between 1793 and 1914.

Recruitment of the fighting forces, 1914–18

Army recruitment, 1914–15

The outbreak of the First World War meant Britain needed to increase its army.

Lord Kitchener's role

In August 1914, Kitchener became Secretary of State for War. Virtually alone among Britain's leaders, he forecast a three- or four-year long war. Realising that Britain would have to put huge armies into the field, he planned accordingly. Given the government's view that conscription would be unpopular, Kitchener had to raise his 'New Armies' by voluntary means.

Recruitment

761,000 recruits joined the army in August and September 1914 and the numbers of volunteers remained high until mid-1915. Codes of patriotism, duty and self-sacrifice, which had permeated every level of society through the education system, youth movements and Sunday schools, underpinned the response. But there were a variety of other motives for the mass enlistment, especially pressure from employers, friends and women.

Pals regiments

On 19 August, General Rawlinson, Director of Recruiting, proposed raising a battalion of London employees who were willing to enlist if 'they were assured that they would serve with their friends'. The War Office approved his proposal. Local corporations, MPs and leading citizens, especially in northern industrial towns, encouraged men who lived in a particular city or who shared a common social and occupational background, to enlist with their 'pals'. By 1 October 1914, 50 pals battalions were complete or in the course of formation.

The composition of the army

Rapid expansion threw together volunteers from all classes, revolutionising the army's social composition. However, the overall patterns of enlistment were uneven:
- Lancashire, Yorkshire and Scotland furnished over one-third of the 250 battalions in Kitchener's first three New Armies: Devon, Dorset, Cornwall and Somerset produced 11 battalions.

- In 1914–15, finance, commerce, the professions and entertainment all contributed over 40 per cent of their pre-war work-force: corresponding returns from manufacturing, transport and agriculture were under 30 per cent.

The shortage of officers

In 1914, only 12,738 regular and 9,563 territorial officers were available. To cater for the infantry battalions raised during 1914–15, Kitchener had to find at least 30,000 more officers. To ease the problem:
- Courses at Sandhurst and Woolwich were shortened.
- Retired officers were brought back into service.
- Temporary commissions were granted.

Conscription

In mid-1915, as army enlistment began to decline, many MPs called for conscription. Prime Minister Asquith initially opposed the idea on the grounds it would undermine traditional liberties and also harm Britain's manufacturing capabilities.

The introduction of conscription

In December 1915, faced with the threat of Lloyd George's resignation, the cabinet accepted conscription for unmarried men and widowers aged 18–41. A Military Service Act, which exempted from conscription the unfit, conscientious objectors, sole supporters of dependents and men engaged on essential war work, became law in January 1916. A second Military Service Act (May 1916) extended liability for military service to all men, single or married, aged 18–41. Conscripted men were recruited for general service and posted to units as required, rather than being raised as distinct formations.

Conscription did not provide more troops. Instead of unearthing 650,000 'slackers', it produced 750,000 new claims for exemption, most of them valid. In the first six months of conscription, average monthly enlistment was less than the rate under the voluntary system. The competing needs of the military and of the war industries remained a contentious issue until November 1918.

Spectrum of significance

Below are a question and a list of general points which could be used to answer the question. Use your own knowledge and the information on the opposite page and on page 74 to reach a judgement about the importance of these general points to the question posed. Write numbers on the spectrum below to indicate their relative importance. Having done this, write a brief justification of your placement, explaining why some of these factors are more important than others. The resulting diagram could form the basis of an essay plan.

To what extent was recruitment a major problem for the British Army in the period 1793–1918?

◄───►

Not a problem   A major problem

1 Harsh discipline and poor pay, 1793–1815

2 The militia, 1793–1815

3 High military death rates, 1815–56

4 Poor barrack facilities, 1815–56

5 The monotony of army life, 1793–1918

6 The prospect of adventure, 1793–1918

7 Imperial pride and patriotism, 1899–1902

8 The rush to enrol, 1914–15

9 Pals regiments, 1914–15

10 The coming of conscription, 1916

 Develop the detail   **a**

Below are a question and a paragraph written as part of an answer to this question. The paragraph contains a limited amount of detail. Annotate the paragraph to add additional detail to the answer.

'In the event of war, the British Army was invariably able to rely on patriotism to attract recruits.' How far do you agree with this statement with regard to the years 1793–1918?

The British Army was not particularly short of recruits in 1916. But many Britons thought that hundreds of thousands of men were 'shirkers' and 'slackers'. Accordingly the government introduced conscription in 1916. Ironically this did not greatly increase the strength of the army.

Exam focus

Below is a sample Section C essay. Read it and the comments around it.

To what extent was Britain successful in recruiting sufficient (non-officer) manpower for its armies in the four major wars in the years 1793–1918?

For almost the entire period of 1793–1918, Britain did not have a system of conscription. Consequently, finding sufficient recruits for the army was a constant problem, particularly when it had to fight countries like France and Germany which had much larger armies. Unable to match such numbers, Britain needed to find allies who could put large armies into the field. It also needed time to raise, train and equip its own forces. The fact that Britain was victorious in the four major wars of the period suggests that its reliance on voluntary recruitment was not misplaced.

In 1793, the British Army amounted to 40,000 men. British public opinion opposed conscription as an imposition on the liberties of freeborn Britons. Finding requisite manpower to take on the military might of France was not easy given that army pay was poor and discipline brutal. Moreover, soldiering was a dangerous profession. Recruiting parties toured the country, trying to encourage support by stressing the prospect of adventure, as well as offering new recruits a bounty of up to £40. Most recruits were from the poorest classes. Soldiers were considered on the same level as common criminals. The army, the Duke of Wellington averred, was 'composed of the scum of the earth'.

Wellington may have been over-stating the case. After 1793, the militia made up a fifth of Britain's land forces. Recruits were selected by ballot and had to serve for five years, with service restricted to home defence. After 1805, as the fears of invasion faded, many militiamen volunteered for regular service, particularly after they were given an extra bounty in 1808. The army also relied on foreign recruitment. When Napoleon occupied Hanover in 1803, many Hanoverians, and men from other German states, made their way to Britain and joined the King's German legion (KGL). Recruits to the KGL soon included Europeans of all descriptions, especially deserters from French armies. By 1813, the army had increased to some 250,000 men, of whom 52,000 were foreign soldiers. Most men were deployed in the defence of Britain and its overseas possessions, Only on one occasion during the French Wars could two British armies of significant size simultaneously be deployed on the continent. In 1809, some 44,000 troops participated in the Walcheran expedition whilst a similar number were in Spain and Portugal.

After 1815, the army was rarely more than 115,000 strong. Long service overseas continued to exact a heavy toll: from 1839–53 there were over 58,000 deaths, mostly due to disease or poorly treated wounds. Manpower problems were compounded by recruitment difficulties. Barracks were overcrowded and insanitary, pay poor, marriage discouraged and discipline harsh. Britain managed to send 26,000 men to the Crimea in 1854, but conditions over the winter of 1854–5 resulted in only 11,000 men being fit for duty by January 1855. The War Office was forced to send militiamen and raw troops to the Crimea and even recruited mercenaries. Efforts were made after 1856 to ensure that Britain had sufficient troops for its own defence. In 1870, the Army Enlistment Act allowed men to sign on for 12 years, notionally six years with the regular army and the rest as part of a reserve force. This act was designed to improve recruitment, but short-term enlistment failed and recruitment remained a major problem.

The introduction focuses well on the set question and provides a guide of the likely direction the essay will take. It makes the essential point that Britain was reliant on voluntary recruitment until 1916.

A well-informed paragraph which establishes the situation in 1793 and examines the problems of recruitment thereafter. It displays good knowledge and good skills of analysis and synthesis. The Wellington quote is effective.

This paragraph challenges Wellington's notion that the army was composed of the 'scum of the earth', and does so convincingly. Impressive knowledge of the French Wars is demonstrated throughout.

A well-balanced paragraph, well geared to the question, which manages to squeeze in many of the recruitment issues between 1815 and 1899.

The army seemed sufficiently large to fight the Boer republics in 1899. Events between October and December 1899 proved that the Boers were a dangerous foe however and, following Black Week, Britons rushed to join the army, as did men from southern Africa, Australia, Canada and New Zealand. In total some 450,000 British and colonial troops served in southern Africa – enough to defeat the Boers. After 1902, Haldane introduced a series of wide-ranging reforms that ensured that Britain had an expeditionary force of 150,000 men ready to fight on the continent. He also established a new territorial force of volunteers, the militia and the yeomanry, which could support and expand the expeditionary force. By 1913, the territorial force had over 200,000 men, providing the framework for a reserve that could be used in the event of war.

That war came in August 1914. Given the government's view that conscription would be nationally divisive, Kitchener had no option but to call for volunteers. Recruitment exceeded all expectations. Some 761,000 recruits joined the army in August and September 1914. The average number of volunteers ran at 125,000 a month until mid-1915. While patriotism probably impelled most men to enlist, other factors also contributed, including the lure of adventure and pressure from peers and women. Northern industrial towns quickly adopted the idea of 'pals' regiments, whereby friends and workmates enlisted and fought together. By the end of September, 50 pals battalions were complete or in the course of formation.

In mid-1915, despite an intensive recruiting campaign, the number of men enlisting in the army began to decline. Faced with the threat of Lloyd George's resignation, Asquith persuaded the cabinet to accept conscription for unmarried men and widowers aged 18–41. The Military Service Act (January 1916) exempted the unfit, conscientious objectors, sole supporters of dependents and men engaged on essential war work. A second Military Service Act (May 1916) extended liability for military service to all men, single or married, aged 18–41. Compulsory service did not achieve its purpose of providing more men for the army. Instead of unearthing 650,000 'slackers', conscription produced 748,587 new claims to exemption, most of them valid, on top of the 1.5 million men already granted immunity by the Ministry of Munitions. In the first six months of conscription, the average monthly enlistment was not much above 40,000 – less than the rate under the voluntary system. Nevertheless, in the last two years of the war, Britain had a continental-sized army fighting on the continent.

Britain relied on voluntary recruitment for all but the last two years of the period 1793–1918, and did so with remarkable success. Its army was strong enough to defeat French forces in the Peninsular War and at Waterloo. Sufficient forces were raised to ensure that Britain played an important military role in the Crimean War. Huge numbers of men volunteered to fight in the Boer War and for two years Britain successfully relied on voluntary recruitment to fight the First World War. Given the relatively small size of its army, Britain was forced to rely heavily on allies in the French Wars, the Crimean War and the First World War. It should be said that if Britain was reliant on allies, those allies were similarly dependent on Britain. It is unlikely that Austria, Russia and Prussia would have defeated Napoleon without British help. France would have struggled to defeat Russia in the Crimea. And the BEF played a decisive role in Germany's defeat in 1918. In short, Britain did enough on the recruitment front to ensure that its army was able to fight successfully in all the major wars of the period.

This paragraph, like the previous paragraphs, displays good skills of analysis and synthesis. It covers the Boer War and the main developments pre-1914.

A detailed paragraph which examines recruitment in 1914. It does so most effectively.

This paragraph examines the introduction of conscription. It makes the essential point that conscription did not have the effect expected.

This is an excellent conclusion. It very much ties in with the introduction and with the issues raised in the course of the essay. It is well written, and displays consistent analysis and understanding of the main issues.

This is a Level 5 essay. It is thorough and detailed, clearly engaging with the question and offering a balanced and carefully reasoned argument, which is sustained throughout the essay. It also shows good skills of analysis and synthesis.

Changing weaponry, 1790-1914

Weaponry development, 1790–1914

Britain's industrial strength ensured that its armed forces were well-equipped.

The navy

The navy led the world in weaponry development.

The French Revolutionary and Napoleonic Wars

Most British ships of the line carried over 70 guns which could fire a cannon ball weighing 32 pounds (14.5 kg). British seamen could unleash a broadside every minute and a half – much faster than their enemies. British ships also had other advantages.

- The carronade, light and able to swivel, was fitted to the **forecastles** and sterns of warships. Nicknamed the 'smasher', it could be fired rapidly. When loaded with **grapeshot**, it made mincemeat of sailors and marines on an opposing ship's upper decks.
- **Gunlocks** replaced **slowmatches**. Slowmatches had to be held against a gun's priming powder, requiring gun captains to position themselves beside the gun and hope the gunpowder ignited and fired. Gunlocks were more efficient because the gun captain stood back from the gun, aimed and (when the time was ripe) yanked on a **lanyard** to set off the firing mechanism. British broadsides thus became faster and more accurate.

Naval developments, 1815–1914

After 1815, there were major changes in warship design and gunnery, ensuring that battleships could fire at enemy ships that were many miles away. Britain usually led the way in naval development. In 1906, for example, it brought into commission the Dreadnought which was faster and better armed than any battleship afloat. Thus began a new phase in the naval arms race. By 1914, Britain's naval budget was twice that of Germany, ensuring that the navy had far more battleships than Germany.

Changing weaponry in the army

The role of science and technology ensured that the British Army often had better weapons than its adversaries.

The French Revolutionary and Napoleonic Wars

Most British soldiers were armed with the reliable Brown Bess musket. Light infantrymen, however, were armed with the Baker rifle. While more difficult to load, it was accurate at up to 200 yards – twice the range of the musket. As well as producing muskets and rifles, Britain had the industrial resources to produce good artillery. Britain also devised two new projectiles.

- Major Henry Shrapnel introduced a new shell. Effective at 700 yards (640 m), it consisted of a metal ball filled with musket balls. It was fused to explode above and in front of its target, spewing the balls and the shell fragments at the enemy.
- Rockets had been used effectively by Indian troops during their wars against the East India Company in the 1790s. Their range was no more than 550 m, but they were improved by William Congreve in England from 1800. By 1806, his rockets had a range of 2700 m. Unfortunately, accuracy was not their strong point and they were rarely used, though they did perform well during the British attack on Copenhagen in 1807.

Developments, 1815–1900

After 1815, British troops usually had better weapons than their enemies. In the Crimean War, for example, British troops had rifled-muskets, much better than the muskets of their Russian opponents.

In the late 1850s, William Armstrong produced a breech-loading and rifled artillery piece, with shells loaded from the rear, not through the muzzle. Adopted by the army in 1859–60, it seemed to inaugurate a new era in artillery technology. However, in 1863 the army decided that that the old guns were superior to Armstrong's guns, since inexperienced gun crews could not reload his weapons at speed. For 17 years, it purchased muzzle-loading artillery rather than Armstrong's guns.

RAG – rate the timeline

Below are a question and a timeline. Read the question, study the timeline and, using three coloured pens, put a Red, Amber or Green star next to the development to show:

Red: Developments that have no relevance to the question

Amber: Developments that have some significance to the question

Green: Developments that are directly relevant to the question

To what extent was the British Army well equipped with weapons in the period 1793–1914?

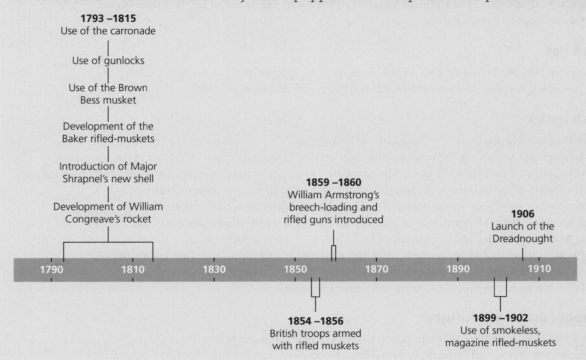

1793 –1815
Use of the carronade

Use of gunlocks

Use of the Brown Bess musket

Development of the Baker rifled-muskets

Introduction of Major Shrapnel's new shell

Development of William Congreave's rocket

1859 –1860
William Armstrong's breech-loading and rifled guns introduced

1906
Launch of the Dreadnought

1790   1810   1830   1850   1870   1890   1910

1854 –1856
British troops armed with rifled muskets

1899 –1902
Use of smokeless, magazine rifled-muskets

Develop the detail   a

Below are a question and the paragraph written as part of an answer to this question. The paragraph contains a limited amount of detail. Annotate the paragraph to add additional detail to the answer.

To what extent did superior weaponry enable Britain to achieve success in the three main wars between 1793 and 1902?

> The winning of naval battles in the French Wars was essentially the result of superior gunnery. The Royal Navy's gunners were better trained than their opponents. They also made use of the carronade and the gunlock. This gave the Royal Navy a huge advantage in battle.

Changing weaponry in the First World War

The impact of the war on land

The war saw important developments in weaponry as the army struggled to meet the challenges of trench warfare.

The Vickers machine-gun, 1914–18

The Vickers machine-gun, which entered service with the army in 1912, soon developed a reputation for reliability. Able to fire 500 rounds a minute, the weapon came in three parts – a mounting tripod, the gun itself and a can of water that fed into the 'water jacket' that surrounded the barrel and stopped it overheating.

Poison gas

The Germans first used chlorine gas in battle in April 1915. The British quickly followed suit. A British gas unit was created which soon developed the far more deadly phosgene.

British tanks

The first tanks, tracked armoured vehicles fitted with armaments, were developed in Britain. The tank's development was partly the responsibility of then navy, largely because First Lord of the Admiralty Churchill backed the project. The first tanks went into action in September 1916 during the Battle of the Somme and, though initially successful in forcing their way through the German trenches, most soon broke down. They had done sufficiently well for more to be ordered, however. By 1917, there were several types of tank, with different armaments and features. As the capabilities and limitations of tanks became better understood, they underwent various modifications and improvements, enabling them to cross the mud and shell-craters of no-man's-land. Tanks had some successes and as many failures. Owing to their mechanical unreliability, they were never able to make a decisive breakthrough.

The importance of artillery

By mid-1918, British artillery was superior to that of Germany. Advances in mapping, aerial photography, surveying and communication helped to produce accurate fire. Artillery, using a variety of specialised shells, became the decisive weapon on the battlefield. The Fuze 106 caused shells to explode on the slightest contact and to expend their blast horizontally, thereby cutting barbed wire.

The importance of aircraft

By 1918, Britain was producing better – and far more – planes than the Germans. Aircraft made a vital contribution to British success on land (see page 60).

Naval developments

Britain retained the upper hand in naval developments. The main threat to Britain's naval dominance came from German **U-boats**. As well as using the convoy system, the navy devised a host of means to deal with the U-boat threat. These included the use of airships and seaplane patrols, new classes of patrol craft and improved depth charges.

Britain's technological role

Churchill viewed the war as an 'engineers' war' in which Allied technology and ingenuity in weapons design was a decisive factor. The Royal Naval Air Service was particularly innovative; its engineers and inventors can claim to have originated tanks and aircraft carriers.

Simple essay style

Below is a sample question. Use your own knowledge and the information on the opposite page and on page 82 to produce a plan for this question. Choose four general points and provide three pieces of specific information to support each general point. Once you have planned your essay, write the introduction and conclusion for the essay. The introduction should list the points to be discussed in the essay. The conclusion should summarise the key points and justify which point was the most important.

To what extent had naval weaponry changed between 1793 and 1918?

 Developing an argument

Below are a question, a list of some of the key points to be made in the essay and a paragraph from the essay. Read the question, the plan and the sample paragraph. Rewrite the paragraph in order to develop an argument. Your paragraph should explain why the factor discussed in the paragraph is either the most significant factor or less significant than another factor.

To what extent did superior weaponry enable the army to defeat its opponents in the four major wars between 1793 and 1918?

Key points
- The French and Napoleonic Wars – weapons or leadership?
- The Crimean War – weapons or allies?
- The Boer War – weapons or superior numbers?
- The First World War – weapons or allies or leadership or superior numbers?

Sample paragraph

By 1918, the British Army was the best in the world. It was also the world's most highly mechanised army. Its overwhelming superiority in technology and war material by August 1918 was the foundation on which Haig built his successful Hundred Days Offensive. Artillery dominance was crucial, including the use of a variety of new shells. The tank, a British invention, also proved its worth. It is, perhaps, the most striking evidence of Britain's ability to integrate science, technology and tactics with greater success than the Germans. However, technological inventiveness by itself could not guarantee victory. For most of the war, the British Army had relied on its allies France and Russia. Without their blood sacrifice, Germany would not have been defeated. By 1918, with the USA's entry into the war, the Allied side had far more men and resources than embattled Germany. Good leadership, by 1918, was also an important factor in the BEF's success.

The population and the war effort

Funding wars

Britain's wealth enabled it to fund – and win – the major wars of the period.

Funding the French Revolutionary and Napoleonic Wars

At least 21 goods and services were newly taxed during the war, including salt, beer, spirits, windows, servants and dogs. In 1799, Parliament imposed a graduated income tax for the first time in Britain's history. Paid by the rich, it raised £155 million by 1815. Before 1793, around £18 million a year was raised in taxes and between 1793 and 1815, an additional £12 million was, on average, extracted every year.

The government also borrowed huge sums of money from merchants and bankers in the City of London. The close relationship between the government and London's powerful capital markets gave Britain a considerable advantage over France.

Financing the Crimean War

Paying for the Crimean War (1853–6) was not a serious problem. It was relatively short and limited in scope and Britain was at the height of its economic power. William Gladstone, Chancellor of the Exchequer in 1854, believed in balancing the budget and reducing taxes. However, the war's costs led to him increasing taxation and increasing the national debt by offering **government bonds** for sale. By contrast, Sir George Cornewall Lewis, who became Chancellor in 1855, believed that heavy taxation was more damaging to the economy than borrowing. He thus borrowed. About half the war's cost was met by government borrowing.

Financing the Boer War

The Boer War cost £217 million. In 1901, Chancellor of the Exchequer Michael Hicks Beach put a tax on refined sugar, imposed a levy of **1s.** on exported coal and raised income tax by 2d in the pound. But the war's cost was mainly met by borrowing by means of bonds and **consols** – only a third was met by taxation.

Financing the First World War

The government initially hoped to pay for the war by borrowing. But the government bonds issued in June 1915 brought in less money than expected.

Increased taxes

To meet the war's costs, Chancellor of the Exchequer Reginald McKenna introduced a war budget in September 1915.
- Income tax increased from 1s.2d to 3s.6d in the pound and the exemption limit was lowered, ensuring people on lower incomes had to pay.
- Supertax rates went up.
- An Excess Profits Duty (EPD) of 50 per cent was imposed on any increase in pre-war profits on all war-related industries.
- High duties were imposed on some 'luxury' articles, for example cars and watches.

The rising cost of the war forced McKenna and his successors to further increase taxes. By 1918, the standard rate of income tax had risen to 6s in the pound. EPD, which rose to 80 per cent in 1917, provided a quarter of the total tax revenue in the war period.

The importance of public borrowing

Despite the increase in taxation, over 30 per cent of war expenditure was met from public borrowing. The payment of interest on the national debt rose from £625 million in 1914 to £7,809 million by 1918. Servicing it took nearly half the yield from taxation in the 1920s.

International finance

Britain was wealthy enough to provide loans totalling £1,825 to its allies. However, it was also forced to raise loans in the USA to pay for vital US supplies. By November 1918, Britain had amassed debts to the USA of about £1,000 million.

! Complete the paragraph   **a**

Below are a question and a paragraph written as part of an answer to the question. The paragraph contains a point and specific examples, but lacks a concluding explanatory link back to the question. Complete the paragraph, adding this link in the space provided.

How successful were Britain's financial policies in meeting the costs of the four major wars between 1793 and 1918?

Given that the Crimean War was relatively short and limited in scope and Britain was at the height of its economic power, paying for the war was not a serious problem. Gladstone, Chancellor of the Exchequer in 1854, believed in balancing the budget and reducing taxes. However, the costs of the war led to him increasing taxation. He was also forced to increase the national debt by offering government bonds for sale. Sir George Cornewall Lewis, Gladstone's successor in 1855, was not particularly concerned about balancing the budget. Convinced that heavy taxation was more damaging to the economy than borrowing, he borrowed. Just under half of the war's cost was ultimately met by government borrowing.

_____

_____

_____

⫶ Spectrum of significance

Below are a question and a list of general points which could be used to answer the question. Use your own knowledge and the information on the opposite page to reach a judgement about the importance of these general points to the question posed. Write numbers on the spectrum below to indicate their relative importance. Having done this, write a brief justification of your placement, explaining why some of these factors are more important than others. The resulting diagram could form the basis of an essay plan.

To what extent was Britain successful in meeting the financial costs of the four main wars between 1793 and 1918?

←——————————————————————————————————→

Less successful   Very successful

Changing cultural roles, 1790–1918

The social impact of war, 1790–1914

Before 1914, wars had only a limited impact on civilians. However, civilians had a major impact on the wars:

- Historian Roger Knight has emphasised the degree to which the efforts of virtually the entire British population contributed to the country's victory in the French Wars.
- In the Crimean War, public opinion, influenced by a powerful press and reporting from the war, helped bring about a change of Prime Minister. Florence Nightingale showed how women could assist the war effort.
- In the Boer War, civilian uproar led to a change in the concentration camp policy.

Camp followers

For most of the period c.1790–1914, women and children followed their husbands/fathers during military campaigns. For many families, the absence of their main wage-earner compelled them to enter the workhouse: most wives chose a life with the forces instead and performed essential duties such as cooking, cleaning and nursing.

Many camp followers became quite wealthy by providing goods, such as alcohol and tobacco, and services, including washing and, of course, prostitution.

The home front

During the French Wars, 1793–1815, militia units were established across the Britain. Their main duty was to maintain law and order during the absence of the regular troops and to suppress outbreaks of unrest. From the 1860s, wealthy pri vate individuals set up volunteer units, providing basic military training.

The impact of the First World War

Most civilians prior to 1914, while generally supporting the war efforts, were not organised for war by the government. This was to change during the First World War.

DORA

The August 1914, the Defence of the Realm Act (DORA) gave the government sweeping power to rule by decree. Its provisions were progressively extended to cover press censorship, requisitioning, control of the sale of alcohol and food regulations.

The Munitions of War Act

The Munitions of War Act (July 1915) gave the Munitions Ministry the power to declare any essential plant a 'controlled establishment' where strikes were banned, fines levied for absenteeism and workers could only move jobs if they received 'leaving certificates'.

Lloyd George

In December 1916, Lloyd George became Prime Minister. Determined to win the war at all costs, he was prepared to suspend traditional liberal 'freedoms' and take greater control of the economy. He created 12 new ministries, including Blockade, Shipping, Food Control, Health and Transport. The new ministries ran what some called '**war socialism**'.

Manpower allocation

In August 1917, General Geddes became Minister of National Service. The coordinated use of mobilised manpower began, a fact underlined by the transfer of control of recruiting from the War Office to the new Ministry (November 1917). Henceforward, the army's manpower demands were accorded a lower priority than those of shipbuilding and aircraft production. In mid-1918, Geddes received powers to allocate labour to particular industries.

The role of women

In 1914, Suffragette groups suspended their campaign for women's right to vote, demanding instead that they be allowed to serve the country by undertaking work that would release men for military duty. Trade union opposition initially made this difficult. But as the labour shortage intensified, women found work and the number of women employed in munitions production rose from 82,859 in 1914 to 947,000 by November 1918. 200,000 women entered government departments. 500,000 took over clerical work in private offices. Female transport workers increased from 18,200 to 117,200.

However, the extent of the changes in women's role can be exaggerated.

- The total number of women doing waged work increased by only 22.5 per cent.
- In 1918, most working women were still employed as domestic servants.

Women's military involvement

The service ministries were reluctant to sanction the use of female personnel. Nevertheless, in 1917, volunteer bodies were consolidated into the Women's Auxiliary Army Corp (WAAC), followed by the Women's Royal Naval Service (WRNS) and later the Women's Royal Air Force (WRAF); in total over 100,000 women. Serving as typists, drivers, clerks and cooks, they released more men for combatant duty. 40,000 women also worked as nurses or female orderlies in Britain or France.

Mind map

Use the information on the opposite page to add detail to the mind map below. This should assist your understanding of the impact of the wars on Britain between 1793 and 1918.

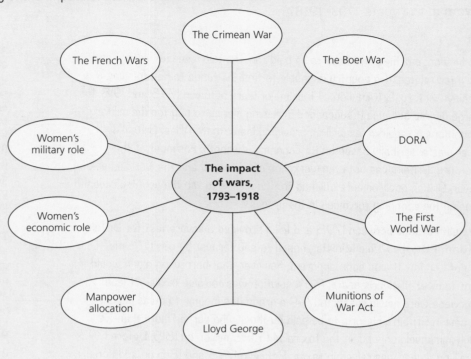

Support or challenge?

Below is a question which asks how far you agree with a specific statement. Below this is a series of general statements which are relevant to the question. Using your own knowledge and the information on the opposite page, decide whether these statements support or challenge the statement to the question and tick the appropriate box.

'The First World War had a greater impact on British civilian life than the combined impact of the French Wars, the Crimean War and the Boer War.' How far do you agree with this statement?

	Support	Challenge
The French Wars had less impact on civilian life than might have been expected.		
The public had more impact on the Crimean War than the war had on the public.		
The Boer War divided – but otherwise did not have too much impact on – civilians.		
DORA gave the government the power to rule by decree.		
The Munitions of War Act reduced munition workers' freedom.		
Asquith's Liberal government opposed too much government intervention.		
By 1918, the Ministry of National Service had the power to allocate labour to particular industries.		
Women's economic role in the First World War was less important than is sometimes thought.		
Women's military role grew in importance in the First World War.		

Exam focus

Below is a high-level essay. Read it and the comments around it.

To what extent did British governments successfully raise money to fund the four major wars in the years 1793–1918?

Wars have to be won, but they also have to be paid for. The two issues – victory and funding – are inter-related. If a country is unable to find the funds to pay for war, it is unlikely to achieve victory. Britain won all four major wars between 1793 and 1918. It did so to a large degree because it succeeded in raising money to pay for the military forces and munitions it required, as well as providing loans to its Allies. Britain's financial power was essentially based on its economic strength. For most of the nineteenth century, Britain was both the workshop of the world and the world's banking house. However, British governments still had to find means to tap the country's wealth without damaging the economy too much in the process.

> A well-focused introduction that highlights several crucial issues, particularly the importance of financial policies. It also gives a good indication of the essay's likely course.

The long wars with France between 1793 and 1815 provided a severe test for Britain. In 1793, William Pitt, the Prime Minister, hoped to pay for war by raising loans from the City of London. It was soon apparent, however, that borrowing alone would be insufficient to meet the war's costs. Pitt's solution was to raise taxes. At least 21 goods and services were newly taxed. In 1799 a graduated income tax was imposed for the first time in Britain's history, to be paid by those who earned more than £60 a year. Though immensely unpopular, the tax raised £155 million by 1815. Before 1793 around £18 million a year was raised in taxes. Between 1793 and 1815 an additional £12 million was extracted on average each year. Pitt's government and those that followed thus deserve credit for their financial policies.

> This paragraph shows impressive powers of synthesis. It also shows detailed knowledge of Pitt's financial policies. The last sentence links back to the introduction/question.

The government, helped by the Bank of England, continued to borrow from the City of London. As the centre of many worldwide markets, no other city in the world had the power and reach of London. A large proportion of government income derived from customs duties, so overseas trade was vital to the war effort. Fortunately, British trade expanded during the war and, by 1815, the value of cotton textiles and manufactured goods was six times greater than in 1793. Britain's growing economy enabled the country to meet the expenses of the Peninsular War and also subsidise their Allies. It is not too much to say that without its strong financial base Britain would not have triumphed against revolutionary France and Napoleon.

> This paragraph deals succinctly with the importance of the City of London and customs duties with regard to money raising. It also touches on the importance of government spending. The last sentence is particularly powerful.

The limited scope of the Crimean War and Britain's position at the height of its economic power, meant paying for the war was not a serious problem. However, the war forced William Gladstone, Chancellor of the Exchequer in 1854, to increase taxation. Income tax rates were doubled and additional revenue raised by increases in stamp duty and duties on spirits, sugar and malt. Gladstone was forced to increase the national debt by offering government bonds for sale. Sir George Cornewall Lewis, who replaced Gladstone in 1855, was convinced that heavy taxation was more damaging to the economy than borrowing, so he borrowed. Just under half the war's cost was met by government borrowing.

> This paragraph demonstrates an excellent understanding of the financial situation between 1854–6.

In the years 1899–1902, Britain had the means to pay for the relatively limited Boer War – a war which cost £217 million. The government met most of the costs by borrowing, but also raised income tax and some indirect taxes.

Financing the First World War was a far greater challenge than the financing of previous wars. A loan, issued in June 1915, brought in only half of the £1,000 million that hoped to have been raised. To meet the war's costs, a war budget was introduced in September 1915 which greatly increased taxes. Income tax went up from 1s. 2d. to 3s. 6d. in the pound. Supertax rates went up and an Excess Profits Duty (EPD) of 50 per cent was imposed on any increase in pre-war profits on all war-related industries. High duties were also imposed on some 'luxury' articles. A huge deficit remained, however, and by 1918 the standard rate of income tax had risen to 6s. in the pound. EPD rose to 80 per cent in 1917. Despite the increase in taxes, less than a third of the national expenditure was met from taxation. Most war expenditure was met from public borrowing, with no limit placed on government borrowing so long as taxation was enough to cover the payment of interest on the national debt. This rose during the war from £625 million to £7,809 million.

Government financial policies, coupled with a shortage of goods, led to inflation. By 1919, the pound bought only a third of what it had done in 1914. Britain could pay for its imports because exports, though much reduced in volume, brought in as much sterling as before the war, due to their increased prices. Britain was thus wealthy enough to provide loans amounting to £1,825 million to its allies. However, the war increased Britain's need for supplies from the USA without increasing British exports to the USA, creating a dollar shortage. This was met partly by raising loans on the American market and partly by sales of American securities held by British citizens. By late 1918, Britain had amassed debts to the USA of about £1,000 million. This debt was far better than defeat by Germany.

Britain paid for its major wars in the period 1793–1918, very successfully, largely thanks to its strong economy. Increased taxation and borrowing did not have a particularly adverse effect on that economy. The fact that it was generally the rich who paid the higher taxes made the wars palatable to ordinary Britons who did not suffer unduly during wartime. Prudent financial policies helped ensure domestic peace and were a major factor in helping to ensure Britain's success in all four major wars.

This paragraph again shows an ability to cut to the chase, focusing on key developments.

A detailed paragraph that shows first-rate knowledge of Britain's financial policies in the First World War.

An important paragraph which again demonstrates the candidate's knowledge and ability to write succinctly. The last sentence is also effective.

The conclusion pulls together the argument that was initiated in the introduction and developed throughout the essay.

This is a Level 5 essay. It demonstrates detailed knowledge of a range of different issues. It also clearly engages with the question, offering a carefully reasoned argument which is sustained throughout the essay.

What makes a good answer?

Use this essay and the comments to make a bullet-pointed list of the characteristics of a Level 5 answer. Use this list when planning and writing your own practice exam essays.

Glossary

1s (one shilling) Twelve old pence or 5 pence in modern money.

Admiralty The body responsible for organising the Royal Navy.

Armistice An agreement to suspend fighting.

Berlin Decrees Napoleon's effort (in 1806) to destroy Britain economically by forbidding Europe to trade with Britain.

Bioscope The first moving film apparatus.

Boer The Dutch word for farmer.

Cholera An infection of the intestine caused by bacteria transmitted in contaminated water. This causes severe vomiting and diarrhoea that can prove fatal.

Combined arms tactics Fighting the enemy by blending together the different branches of the army, for example, artillery, infantry and tanks.

Commando An armed group of Boers varying in size from a few dozen men to several hundred.

Commissariat The body responsible for supplying the army with food and other basic necessities.

Consols Government-issued securities that people could buy. Unlike war bonds, no date was stipulated for the return of the capital investment.

Continental System A name for Napoleon's effort to block trade with Britain after 1806.

Creeping barrage An artillery bombardment, where the shells are meant to keep falling just ahead of the attacking troops.

D-Notice system Instructions sent by the government to newspapers, ordering them not to publish certain information. D is short for defence.

Division A formation usually comprising 4,000-5,000 soldiers.

Dysentery An infection of the bowel causing painful diarrhoea. This can be fatal. Dysentery occurs where there is poor sanitation.

Forecastle The raised deck at the front of a ship.

French Revolution The term used to describe the political turbulence in France between 1789–94.

GHQ General Head Quarters, comprising military staff officers who advised the Commander-in-Chief on policy and administration and helped him to carry out his plans.

Gotha The main German bomber.

Government bonds Securities issued by the government, allowing it to borrow money. Those who bought the bonds were guaranteed to receive their money back in the future.

Grapeshot Iron shot contained in a canvas bag that scattered widely when fired.

Guerrillas Irregular forces that harass an enemy. The word was coined by the Spanish during the Peninsular War.

Gunlock The mechanism in some guns by which the charge is exploded.

Hanover A small German state.

Hindenburg Line A heavily fortified German defence system, prepared over the winter of 1916–17.

Lanyard A short piece of rope.

Magazine rifle A rifle which can fire a succession of shots without reloading.

Nore The area at the mouth of the River Thames.

Petty officers Seamen who were not commissioned officers but who had some authority.

Portuguese East Africa Present-day Mozambique.

Rifled musket These weapons had grooved barrels, ensuring that they were more accurate than the smoothbore musket.

Salient A bulge pushing into enemy lines which could thus be attacked from several sides.

Scorched earth The policy of destroying everything that may be of use to an enemy army.

Scurvy A disease caused by a lack of vitamin C.

Ships of the line The main battleships in the French Wars, 1793–1815.

Slowmatch A slow-burning rope used for firing a gun.

Staff work Planning and organisation undertaken by officers working with the Army Commander-in-Chief.

Stern The back of a ship.

Typhoid A disease contracted by drinking infected water.

Typhus A dangerous fever transmitted by lice, fleas, mites or ticks.

U-boats German submarines.

Veldt Open grass country.

Volunteers Men with some basic military training who could be called on to fight if Britain was invaded.

War socialism The government's control of many aspects of British economic and social life during the First World War.

Yeomanry Volunteer cavalry who served in Britain.

Key figures

Sir Winston Churchill (1874–1965) Churchill, a famous war correspondent in the Boer War, became a Conservative MP in 1900. In 1904, he joined the Liberal party because he opposed tariff reform. From 1908–22, he served as President of the Board of Trade, Home Secretary, First Lord of the Admiralty, Minister of Munitions, Secretary of State for War and Colonial Secretary. In 1924, he became Conservative Chancellor of the Exchequer. He was at odds with his party for most of the 1930s over its policies with regard to India and Germany. From 1940–45, he led Britain during the Second World War. He returned as Conservative Prime Minister in 1951, serving until his resignation in 1955.

Douglas Haig (1861–1928) Haig remains one of Britain's most controversial military leaders. Having seen active service in Sudan and in the Boer War, he became Director of Military Training in 1906. In 1915, he became Commander-in-Chief of the BEF. He directed the Battle of the Somme (1916), was appointed Field Marshal and directed the Battle of Passchendaele (1917). In 1918, he led the Hundred Days Offensive which won the First World War.

Emily Hobhouse (1860–1926) A British welfare campaigner, Hobhouse is primarily remembered for bringing to the attention of the British public the atrocious conditions in the concentration camps in southern Africa. She worked hard to improve the situation in the camps in 1901–2.

Horatio Herbert Kitchener (1850–1916) After service with the Royal Engineers, Kitchener was appointed to the Egyptian Army (1883), becoming Commander-in-Chief in 1892. In 1898, he won the Battle of Omdurman and became Governor-General of the Sudan. Replacing Roberts as Commander-in-Chief of the British Army in the second Boer war, he suppressed the Boer guerrillas by a scorched earth policy and by the internment of civilians in concentration camps. As War Secretary (1914), his recruitment campaign was hugely successful. He drowned on his way to Russia in 1916.

David Lloyd George (1863–1945) A Radical Liberal MP, Lloyd George gained fame by his opposition to the Boer War. He became Chancellor of the Exchequer in 1908 and was responsible for introducing old-age pensions. In 1915 he became a dynamic Minister of Munitions. In 1916, he was Secretary of State for War and then Prime Minister. Devious, unscrupulous and delighting in improvisation, he proved a great war leader. Without his leadership, Britain might well have lost the First World War.

Horatio Nelson (1758–1805) Nelson, who took command of his first ship at the age of 21, was probably Britain's greatest ever naval commander. Having lost the sight in his right eye and his right arm in action, he won the battles of the Nile (1798), Copenhagen (1801) and Trafalgar (1805). He died at Trafalgar. He was a naturally gifted commander who inspired men and fellow officers, winning their trust, respect and affection.

Florence Nightingale (1820–1910) In spite of family opposition, Nightingale decided to make her career in nursing, in 1844. She became a national heroine for her work in the Crimean War. Despite being intermittently bedridden and depressed, she continued to promote the development of nursing and hospital reform after 1856. In 1859, she published the influential book *Notes on Hospitals*. In 1860, she set up the Nightingale Training School at St Thomas's Hospital in London.

Henry John Temple, Viscount Palmerston (1784–1865) Palmerston entered parliament as a Tory in 1807, serving as Secretary for War from 1809–28. By 1830, he had joined the Whigs and was a belligerent and nationalistic foreign secretary for most of the 1830s and 1840s. He replaced Lord Aberdeen as Prime Minister in 1855 during the Crimean War. He proved to be a popular leader. Although he had to step down in 1858, he returned as Prime Minister in 1859, serving until his death.

William Pitt (1759–1806) Known as Pitt the Younger (his father, also called William is known as Pitt the Elder), he became Prime Minister in 1783 – the youngest in British history. He served as Prime Minister until 1801 and then again from 1804–6. He proved himself to be a capable if not inspiring war leader. His great strength lay in the realm of finance. He ensured that Britain was able to pay for the French Wars, introducing the income tax in 1799.

FitzRoy James Henry Raglan (1788–1855) Raglan served under Wellington in the Napoleonic Wars, losing an arm at the battle of Waterloo. He became Wellington's secretary, succeeding him as Master General of the Ordnance in 1852. In 1854, he became Commander in the Crimean War. His leadership was much criticised, especially over the winter of 1854–5. The Raglan sleeve, extending to the neck without shoulder seams, is named after him.

Frederick Sleigh Roberts (1832–1914) Born in India, Roberts proved himself an outstanding soldier during the Indian Mutiny (1857–8), winning the Victoria Cross for bravery. He greatly enhanced his military reputation during the second Afghan War (1878–80). He crowned his career with victory as Commander-in-Chief (1899–1900) of British forces in the second Boer War. A grateful Parliament awarded him £100,000 as a reward for his work.

William Howard Russell (1820–1907) Born in Ireland, Russell was a popular reporter with *The Times*. He spent 22 months covering the Crimean War in 1854–5 and is often considered to be the first modern war correspondent. He later covered the American Civil War (1861–5), the Austro-Prussian War (1866) and the Franco-Prussian War (1870–1).

Mary Seacole (1805–81) Daughter of a Scottish army officer and a Jamaican woman, she has become almost as famous as Nightingale for her nursing work during the Crimean War. She is generally praised today for her achievements in overcoming the racial and gender prejudices of many sections of Victorian society. Her nursing achievements were far less considerable than those of Nightingale.

Jan Smuts (1870–1950) Following a brilliant undergraduate career at Cambridge University, Smuts – a Boer – returned as a lawyer to Cape Town in 1895. He was a successful commando leader in the Boer War but thereafter worked for reconciliation with Britain. He became a minister in the South African government in 1910. He was a member of Lloyd George's imperial war cabinet in 1917–18 and helped establish the League of Nations. He was South African Prime Minister from 1919–24. He became Prime Minister of South Africa again in 1939 and supported South Africa's entry into the Second World War.

Arthur Wellesley, Duke of Wellington (1769–1851) Wellington was probably Britain's greatest army commander. Joining the army in 1787, he first made his military reputation in India winning the battles of Assaye and Argaum. He later led British forces to victory in the Peninsular War (1808–14) and finally defeated Napoleon at the battle of Waterloo (1815). He went on to serve as Prime Minister (1828–30).

Timeline

1793	France declared war on Britain
1794	Battle of the Glorious First of June
1797	Battle of Cape St Vincent
	Naval mutinies at Spithead and the Nore
	Battle of Campberdown
1798	Battle of the Nile
1799	Introduction of Income Tax
1799–1800	The Combination Acts
1801	Battle of Copenhagen
1802–3	Peace of Amiens
1805	Battle of Trafalgar
1808	Start of the Peninsular War
1809	Retreat from Corunna
	Battle of Talavera
1811–12	Luddite action in the Midlands and northern England
1812	Battle of Salamanca
1813	Battle of Vitoria
1815	Battle of Waterloo
1854	Britain and France declared war on Russia
	Battle of Alma
	Battle of Balaclava, including Charge of the Light Brigade
	Florence Nightingale arrived at Scutari
	Battle of Inkerman
1855	Lord Aberdeen resigned
	Palmerston became Prime Minister
	Fall of Sebastopol
1856	Treaty of Paris
1868–74	Cardwell's military reforms
1899	Start of the Second Boer War
	Black Week
1900	Battle of Spion Kop
	Relief of Kimberley, Ladysmith and Mafeking
	Khaki election
1901	Concentration camp scandal
1902	End of the Second Boer War
1906	Launch of the Dreadnought
1907	Territorial Army created
1914	Britain declared war on Germany
	Defence of the Realm Act
	First Battle of Ypres
1915	Allied landings at Gallipoli
	Lloyd George became Minister of Munitions
	Munitions of War Act
	McKenna War Budget
1916	Battle of Jutland
	Battle of the Somme
	Lloyd George became Prime Minister
1917	Germany renewed unrestricted submarine warfare
	Battle of Arras
	Third Battle of Ypres (Passchendaele)
1918	Ludendorff Spring Offensive
	Formation of the RAF
	Hundred Days Offensive
	Armistice

Mark schemes

AO1 mark scheme

- **Analytical focus**
- **Accurate detail**
- **Supported judgement**
- Argument and structure

AS		A-Level
1–4	Level 1 ● **Simplistic, limited focus** ● **Limited detail, limited accuracy** ● **No judgement or asserted judgement** ● Limited organisation, no argument	1–3
5–10	Level 2 ● **Descriptive, implicit focus** ● **Limited detail, mostly accurate** ● **Judgement with limited support** ● Basic organisation, limited argument	4–7
11–16	Level 3 ● **Some analysis, clear focus (maybe descriptive in places)** ● **Some detail, mostly accurate** ● **Judgement with some support, based on implicit criteria** ● Some organisation, the argument is broadly clear	11–16
17–20	Level 4 ● **Clear analysis, clear focus (maybe uneven)** ● **Sufficient detail, mostly accurate** ● **Judgement with some support, based on valid criteria** ● Generally well organised, logical argument (may lack precision)	13–16
	Level 5 ● **Sustained analysis, clear focus** ● **Sufficient accurate detail, fully answers the question** ● **Judgement with full support, based on valid criteria (considers relative significance)** ● Well organised, logical argument communicated with precision	17–20

AO2 mark scheme

Level	Marks	Description
1	1–3	Surface level comprehension of the Source, demonstrated by quoting or paraphrasing, without analysis
		Some relevant knowledge of the historical context is included, but links to the Source are limited
		Either no overall evaluation of the Source, or discussion of reliability and utility is very basic
2	4–7	Some understanding of the Source, demonstrated by selecting and summarising relevant information
		Some relevant knowledge of the historical context is added to the Source to support or challenge the detail it includes
		An overall judgement is presented, but with limited support. Discussion of reliability and utility are based on a limited discussion of provenance and may reflect invalid assumptions
3	8–12	Understanding of the Source, demonstrated by some analysis of key points, explaining their meaning and valid inferences
		Relevant knowledge of the historical context is used to support inferences. Contextual knowledge is also used to expand on, support, or challenge matters of detail from the Source
		An overall judgement is presented, which relates to the nature and purpose of the Source. The judgement is based on valid criteria, but the support is likely to be limited.
4	13–16	Analysis of the Source, demonstrated by examining their evidence to make reasoned inferences. Valid distinctions are made between information and opinion. Treatment of the two enquiries may be uneven
		Relevant knowledge of the historical context is used to reveal and discuss the limitations of Source's content. The answer attempts to interpret the Source material in the context of the values and assumptions of the society it comes from
		Evaluation of the Source reflects how much weight the evidence of the Source can bear. Evaluation is based on valid criteria. Aspects of the judgement may have limited support
5	17–20	Confident interrogation of the Source, in relation to both enquiries, demonstrated by reasoned inferences. The answer shows a range of ways the Source can be used, making valid distinctions between information and opinion
		Relevant knowledge of the historical context is used to reveal and discuss the limitations of Source's content. The answer interprets the Source material in the context of the values and assumptions of the society it comes from
		Evaluation of the Source reflects how much weight the evidence of the Source can bear and may distinguish between the degrees to which aspects of the Source can be useful. Evaluation is based on valid criteria

Notes

Quick quizzes at www.hoddereducation.co.uk/myrevisionnotes